W9-BXN-893

The Kitchen Classroom

LA CROSSE COUNTY LIBRARY

The Kitchen Classroom

32 Visual GFCF Recipes to Boost Developmental Skills

Gabrielle Kaplan-Mayer

Woodbine House   2010

641.563
Ka
c.1

© 2010 Gabrielle Kaplan-Mayer

All rights reserved under International and Pan-American copyright conventions. Published in the United States of America by Woodbine House, Inc., 6510 Bells Mill Rd., Bethesda, MD 20817. 800-843-7323. www.woodbinehouse.com

Library of Congress Cataloging-in-Publication Data

Kaplan-Mayer, Gabrielle.
 The kitchen classroom : 32 visual GFCF recipes to boost developmental skills / Gabrielle Kaplan-Mayer.
     p. cm.
 Includes bibliographical references and index.
 ISBN 978-1-60613-010-0
 1. Developmentally disabled children—Rehabilitation. 2. Cooking for children with mental disabili-
ties. 3. Cooking—Therapeutic use. I. Title.
 HV891.K37 2010
 649'.63—dc22

                                                                                            2010036850

Printed in USA
10 9 8 7 6 5 4 3 2 1

Dedication

For George and June—who open my heart every day.

Table of Contents

Acknowledgments

Seeing *The Kitchen Classroom* reach publication is the result of so many people supporting and helping me to create this manuscript:

My deepest appreciation goes to my friend, Jennifer Paget, who has been working with my husband, Fred, and me as my son George's RDI consultant for over three years. In that time, her ongoing guidance and insights have helped us to help George learn and grow in so many ways. Without her vision, I may have never tried cooking with George!

My husband, Fred, is not only an incredible partner, but also an incredible parent. His belief in and support of my creative work has no limits—even when it means our sink is ever full of dirty dishes! During the picture taking process for this book, Fred was a calm, centered presence who helped our kids take their turns and wait patiently in between pictures!

Photographer Sandra Segal is incredible at what she does—as you will see when you check out the photos in this book and CD-ROM. Sandy's open, joyful, generous energy made my children feel instantly comfortable in her presence. Thank you, Sandy.

When I first mailed my manuscript to Woodbine House, I had no idea that it would fall into the hands of an editor who immediately understood my vision. It was true grace and synchronicity that Editor Nancy Gray Paul read my work and began to think creatively about how my ideas could be turned into the best product possible for parents, teachers, and children. I am grateful for all of her energy and support in making *The Kitchen Classroom* come to be.

Finally, I want to thank my wonderful children, George and June, for learning with and teaching me in so many ways.

—Gabrielle Kaplan-Mayer

Introduction

Welcome! I am so delighted that you've picked up ***The Kitchen Classroom*** and hope that it will inspire you on your cooking journey with your children, whether you are new to cooking, an experienced cook, or a parent or teacher of a child with or without special needs. This is more than just a cookbook; it is a guide for creating shared experiences and lasting memories with your child while encouraging optimal nutrition and developing your child's social, motor, and cognitive skills.

As I see it, cooking with young children is a way to slow down and exhale. It is a way to instill respect for health and a connection to the earth and to animals—where our food comes from. Cooking with young children is also an excellent way to teach language, math, and sequential thinking. But most important of all, cooking with your children is a way of being present with them, of sharing experiences that they will internalize and remember. Using this book, I hope you'll discover, as I have, that cooking with kids is a fun and natural way to connect, communicate, *and* teach skills!

I've divided ***The Kitchen Classroom*** into three parts for your convenience. The first part of the book contains chapters with information about the process of cooking with young children (even as young as eighteen months), how to successfully prepare for the experience, and how to ensure you all get the most out of it. The introductory chapters are short and easy to read and I recommend that you start there first so you'll have a game plan before jumping into cooking.

In the next section you will find thirty-two recipes written for you—the adult. Every one of these recipes is gluten-free (GF) and has the potential to be casein-free (GFCF) as well (substitutions are provided where necessary). Each recipe is rated by level of difficulty: Level I (easy), Level 2 (moderately difficult), Level III (more difficult), and each section begins with the most basic recipes. Included is a list of the ingredients and cooking tools you'll need to make each dish. The recipes are broken down into steps, just like in a typical cookbook, but in *The Kitchen Classroom* the steps are marked with symbols. Each symbol represents the particular skill set that you and your child will apply to that step in the cooking process (see the Symbol Key on page 35). In other words, the symbols will let you know which steps are opportunities to practice literacy, math, science, fine and gross motor skills; which steps provide sensory input; and which steps are occasions to develop language, communication, and social skills. An overall symbol has been assigned to each recipe that represents the skill set your child will be focusing in on the most during the process of making that dish. Depending on your child's developmental stage, you may choose to focus on one set of skills at a time or work on different skills within the process of cooking a single dish. Only carry out as many of the suggestions in the adult instructions as you and your child can handle. Also included in this book are color photos of each of the prepared dishes. Use these to whet your child's appetite and select which recipe you'll cook next.

Specifically for your children, I've created a CD-ROM that contains photos and basic written instruction for each step in each recipe. Using this, you and your kids can follow along with me and my kids as we cook. This feature—which is essentially an activity schedule—is wonderful for visual learners! Whether your children are readers or emergent readers, the written text along with each photo will help support the experiential learning process.

The true benefit of all of this being on a CD-ROM is that it is yours to customize to your child's specific needs. You can delete steps if the instructions are too simplified for your child (e.g., your child already knows to wash his hands before starting to cook), or you can edit recipes to include different ingredients (i.e., your child can't tolerate chocolate chips so you substitute raisins). Following our design, you can even take pictures of your *own* child in the kitchen and insert them to make the recipes feature your kid!

Once you're ready to get cooking, set your laptop on the kitchen counter and scroll through the photos as you and your child work. Or you may decide to print out the photos and instructions, spread them out on the counter, and let them get messy as you cook. Or laminate them and place them in a special binder for repeated use. They are yours and I am confidant that each of you will find the best way to make them work for your family.

So, thank you for joining me in **The Kitchen Classroom**! Will you let me know how your cooking experiences are going? Please ask any questions, too. You can find me at www.kitchenclassroom4kids.com.

Happy cooking!

Chapter 1
Cooking as a Shared Experience

When I was growing up, the best cook that I knew was my grandmother. She lived five hours away from us, but when she came to visit, she would load up her Buick's trunk with coolers full of her roasts and soups and cakes. She would take over my mother's kitchen—there would be no microwave dinners while Grandma was around. I loved to watch her cook and take in the smells that filled our kitchen. Grandma would put a spoon in my hand and have me stir batter while she beat the eggs for meringue; she would hand me carrots to peel while she worked on potatoes and then we'd throw them together into her giant, black soup pot. As I grew older, Grandma let me do more cooking until it got to the point where I would kick her out of the kitchen and make her a "surprise" meal. I was a teenager by then and Grandma respected my independence and was a great sport about trying all of my "concoctions," as she liked to call them.

These childhood memories of being in the kitchen with Grandma stand out from the others not only because of the way that my grandmother transmitted family recipes, culture, and tradition as well as culinary skills, but also because these are the moments that I remember just *being* together. Cooking was our special time—our shared experience. When we were cooking together, we talked and laughed; we played and anticipated what would come out of the oven. (By the way, though my grandmother passed away in 2007 at age ninety-five, I still use her pots and pans daily and think of her when I cook.)

This practice of sharing time in the kitchen is an ancient one. In every culture, people (generally women) in the family share the work of preparing meals together, passing along knowledge, family secrets, and stories in the process. For many modern families, especially those with two parents who work outside of the home, it is hard to make time for cooking. Dinner is often carry-out or something that comes from the freezer and gets popped into the microwave. Not only is our culture seeing serious health ramifications as a result of feeding children primarily processed food (including childhood obesity and a rising incidence of type 2 diabetes in children), but we are also facing a serious cultural and emotional dearth for our children who don't get to experience the process of creating food with the family and for the family.

Rather than focusing on blame or despair for these conditions, I prefer to advocate for the simple pleasure of making a little bit of time in your life to cook healthy food with your children. **Please don't feel guilty if this isn't something that you do regularly**—all of us are juggling so much to keep up with the demands of our daily lives. For parents who are pressed between the responsibilities of work and home, cooking *with* your children rather than just *for* them is a way to make space for quality time. *The Kitchen Classroom* is about creating space in your life—it may be daily or weekly or once or twice a month—when you and your child can step away from the demands of the outside world and just be together in the warmth of your kitchen. (That you are creating healthy food and teaching your child important cognitive skills while you cook is another bonus, and will be discussed in the following chapters.)

Fostering Social Skills through Cooking

Although I enjoyed cooking as a child and now work professionally as a cooking instructor, I did not begin cooking with my children until my son, George, was four and newly diagnosed with autism. Like many parents facing this news, my husband and I despaired and worried that his impaired communication and relational skills would prevent him from learning and developing. We began using a cognitive-developmental therapy with him called Relationship Development Intervention (RDI), which teaches parents how to help their children with autism develop "dynamic intelligence." Dynamic intelligence is a collection of specific cognitive, self-regulatory, interpersonal, and communication abilities that allow us to respond and adapt to a complex world—things that do not come naturally to people with autism. Dynamic intelligence provides us with the tools to organically respond to what is happening in our environment in the moment—rather than responding to social situations with scripted behaviors.

One of the foundational approaches to developing dynamic intelligence in RDI is creating shared experience between the child and her parents—something that is not easy when a child's natural inclination is to retreat into repetitive patterns rather than engaging, even with parents. One of the first activities that our RDI consultant, Jennifer Paget, engaged George in was cooking. They made edible gluten-free play dough and cookies. (By this point we had begun George on the gluten-free/casein-free diet that is so helpful to many children with autism.) I was amazed to see how much George engaged in cooking with Jennifer and how his attention—which usually moved from one thing to another very rapidly—stayed with her while they cooked.

After witnessing this, I started cooking with George at home, and what has developed is a wonderful routine that we share several times a week when we stir, pour, cut, even break eggs as a team. Not only has cooking given us a way to connect, it has also increased George's cognitive abilities and inspired greater confidence. At age seven, George can now follow familiar recipes almost independently.

I also cook with my daughter June, age four, and with George and June together. This is an excellent opportunity for sibling bonding. For more social skills practice, you might consider inviting one of your child's classmates or neighbors over for a cooking play date. Using cooking as a framework or structure for social interaction provides practice for turn-taking, sharing, patience, cooperation, and takes the pressure off of both children and allows for more spontaneous communicating.

If you will be cooking with more than one child, think about giving each child a role in the cooking process. For example, when making cookies, I will set up certain things for June to pour and certain things for George to pour and we'll all take turns stirring. In fact, while one of them is stirring, the other child and I will pantomime the motions for extra practice. We also make sure to count as we cook, for example, "one, two, three shakes of salt," which we all say together. In this way, we foster independence while building a sense of camaraderie.

In addition to cooking with my kids and their friends, and I also cook with classes of five-, six-, and seven-year-olds at a local synagogue, and with groups of teenagers with disabilities and learning differences, who make meals every month for elderly people who are no longer able to cook for themselves. I have seen the way that being part of a cooking class has helped each one of these students to grow in profound ways, especially socially.

Lee, who has Down syndrome, began cooking with me at age sixteen and just celebrated his nineteenth birthday. When he first started in our cooking class, I would ask another student to work alongside him to make sure that he was safe doing tasks that required fine motor skills, especially cutting. With each month that went by and the cutting practice that went with it, Lee began to greatly improve his fine motor skills and went from using a butter knife to a small chopping knife. His ability to follow the step-by-step sequence of a recipe also improved. He requested that our class make a chocolate raspberry cake to celebrate his eighteenth birthday. On the week before his birthday, I assembled all of the ingredients and when Lee entered the classroom, I assigned him the job of making the whole cake on his own. With minimal assistance from me to make sure that he understood and was moving from step to step in the recipe, Lee baked his own chocolate raspberry birthday cake, which came out wonderfully and the whole class enjoyed!

Heather has been in my cooking class for three years and has just turned seventeen. Heather has an intellectual disability (ID) and does not read. She is a self-proclaimed "social butterfly," which is an accurate portrayal. Of all the jobs in our cooking class, Heather loves baking the most. When she comes into class, I show her what we will be baking and she helps me to gather all of the ingredients from the pantry. Working with a peer, Heather has learned the skills needed to make all kinds of cookies and cakes: creaming butter, rolling cookie balls, dusting with sugar, setting a timer, pricking the center of a cake with a toothpick to see if it comes out moist, etc. Because Heather is not mainstreamed in her public school, our cooking class is one of the few opportunities that she has to interact with typically developing peers and she talks about her two sets of friends, those from school and those from cooking class.

Jake is sixteen and has been cooking with me for two years. He has a PDD (Pervasive Developmental Disorder) diagnosis and struggles with issues of attention and impulsivity. He comes to class with an aide who is largely there to take him home when he has no more attention for cooking. Our class is two hours long, which includes an introduction to what we will be cooking; special instruction about techniques that we will be using; cooking time; a short lesson about food, cooking, or nutrition; tasting time; and packing the food for the elderly residents for whom we prepare it.

When Jake first came to class, I knew that he would get fidgety during my introduction, so I would have some task set aside for him to work on right away. His attention generally lasted until it was time for our lesson and then he would want to leave. In the last six months, I have noticed that Jake is able to stay for more class time, particularly if I can entice him to sample what we've cooked (he used to have no interest in tasting the food). His aide takes more of a backseat and Jake has gradually gone from needing some special instruction to more or less doing what his peers are doing. His attention is better focused on some days than others, but that is not terribly different from the other fifteen-year-old boys who take part in the class.

Each of these students has improved their skills in the kitchen, but perhaps even more importantly, has grown in their sense of being part of the group. Each student has increased their attention span and has acquired abilities that will help them to become more independent adults, whether they ultimately live alone or in a supported environment.

With each student, it was critical that I met them where they were when they first began cooking with me. That meant that Lee needed to use a knife that he could handle, that Heather did not have to read a recipe, and that Jake was engaged in hands-on learning and not expected to sit still during lecture time. By meeting them where they were, I was able to frame their cooking experience so that they could learn and grow, which each of them has done beautifully.

Chapter 2
Cooking with Children with Developmental Disabilities

If you are a parent or educator of children who have developmental or learning challenges, I guarantee that cooking with them will create an opportunity for them to learn and grow. I have seen firsthand how cooking not only strengthens the relationship between me and my son, but allows him to connect with peers, friends, and cousins.

To ensure that cooking is a successful experience for children with developmental or learning differences, keep the following in mind:

1. **Your child or students may need more practice** than their typically developing peers. Spend time doing lots of repetitive tasks that will build motor skills, like slicing a banana with a butter knife. With practice, you will be able to gradually increase the cooking challenges.

2. **Your child or students may benefit from special instruction,** like following along with the pictures in *The Kitchen Classroom* CD-ROM, as opposed to reading the words in the recipes if they are not yet reading or if reading is a challenge.

3. **Your child or students may have limited attention** and so to build attention, start with short activities. You may cook together for five minutes and make a quick, easy recipe like "Tasty Trail Mix." The first few times that you cook together, they may only attend for five minutes, but as they get comfortable and you add more challenges, five minutes will become eight minutes and then ten minutes, and so forth. Meet the children where they are and build slowly from there. Only carry out as many of the suggestions in the adult instructions as you and your

children or students can manage. Take a deep breath, let them make a mess, look for opportunities for learning, and enjoy the process!

4. **Your child or students may struggle with sharing and cooperating** with others, so consider where you can highlight a turn-taking component to the recipe. Maybe one child stirs five times and then another stirs five times and you go back and forth like this. As comfort with sharing and cooperating in the kitchen increases, you can invite a peers, siblings, cousins, or grandparents to join you in the kitchen.

5. **Your child or students may need to go at a slower pace than typically developing children** and that is just fine. Be aware of your own pacing and energy. Notice if when you slow down your pace your child becomes more attentive, engaged, or relaxed. If it takes twenty minutes to wash and break celery stalks, that is just fine. It is twenty minutes that you and your child are engaging in together. Moving at a slower pace can give your child more time to process each step and follow what you are modeling.

6. **Your child may need you to set very clear limits,** especially when it comes to safety (see more on this topic below). Set the environment up for cooking (more in a later chapter) so that your materials and utensils are ready for you to use but are out of your child's reach. Be clear and firm as you set limits around cooking and safety. Children will go through developmental stages around limit setting and testing, so stay tuned in to your child moving through stages. I never worry now that George will dump out ingredients (thank goodness!) but I am watchful that he won't try to sneak certain favorite ingredients to snack on while we're cooking. (Annoying as this phase is, I can appreciate his developmental growth in that he's consciously planning how to sneak the snack!)

7. **Your child or students may be tired, not feeling well, or just not in the mood to cook some days** and that's okay! I know that like many moms of kids with ASD, I need to tune into George's energy because it is difficult for him to express exactly what he's feeling. There are days when his vibe is clear that he just isn't up to cooking and I don't force the experience. His energy naturally returns on another day and the opportunity for cooking is there for us.

Chapter 3
"Framing" the Experience for Success

One of the most important things that my husband and I have learned from doing RDI therapy with our son is the concept of "framing." Framing is a dynamic process. It involves thinking about your child's developmental level and setting up the environment and circumstances so that he is most likely to have a successful experience. Framing an activity requires that you, as a parent, think through all of the important elements of an activity before diving in, including the length of the activity, how the room is set up, and what role your child and others will be playing in the activity. Each time that you plan an activity, you "frame" it so your child will focus his attention on a specific skill.

For young children and those with disabilities, it is essential to plan ahead and "frame" activities in a way that is appropriate to their particular developmental level. You'll need to take into account their attention and motor planning issues as well as language delays. The goal is to orchestrate the activity in a way that allows the child to feel confident and competent. When I think about starting a cooking activity with George, I think about what parameters I need to set up to help him focus his attention (an ongoing issue for him). For example, I have discovered that if we are working on a countertop cluttered with lots of mail and other junk, the visual distraction prevents George from focusing on what ingredients need to go into the mixing bowl. But by thinking ahead and creating a work space for us that is clear of clutter, I am able to help George focus better and work effectively. I have discovered that the same is true for my daughter, June, who is developing typically but is younger. (Heck—it works better for me too!)

Kids who have motor planning difficulties benefit from framing as well. As a parent, consider what activities will help your child develop her motor skills and what activities might be too challenging. Begin with activities that she is able to do successfully in order to build up her confidence and then slowly introduce the challenge of more difficult tasks. You might work on certain motor skills like stirring using hand-over-hand guidance at first and then move on to letting your child stir on her own as she develops more strength and agility in stirring.

For a child who has language delays, you can frame activities to help him work on language and communication skills while you cook together. For example, you might work on making simple choices by using visual cues as you cook together. You can ask your child whether he prefers to use a blue or red bowl while you hold up both, or if he'd rather add nuts or raisins to the cookie batter while you point to them on the counter. Think about what language concepts you want to work on—from as basic as answering a yes or no question to as complex as a vocabulary list of exotic ingredients—and how you can bring that lesson into your cooking time.

Framing Your Cooking Experience

Before you begin cooking, take a look around your kitchen and take stock (no pun intended!) of how ready you are to cook. Each recipe in *The Kitchen Classroom* begins by listing both the ingredients and tools that you will need for your cooking experience. Before looking through your drawers, cabinets, and pantry, take some time to look at the big picture of your kitchen. Ask yourself the following questions to help you pre-plan or frame your cooking activity for optimal success:

- *How can I make my space/environment work best for the cooking activity*? I don't have a big, wide open kitchen with lots of counter space. What that means for me is that I need to take time to clear clutter from my counters before bringing in my children to cook. We prefer using our dining room table for cooking preparation when we need to spread out a lot of ingredients and utensils. I also turn on as many lights as I can so things are clearly visible. You might turn off music or the television if your child is distracted by these things. Conversely, turn on the radio if your child is energized by bopping along to music as he cooks.

- *What utensils and cookware will I need?* Refer to the list of all the "tools" you'll need for each recipe right beside the ingredient list. Most of these recipes rely on the basics: you'll want to have a couple of big bowls ready as well as measuring cups and spoons. Make sure that everything is easily accessible and kid-friendly (e.g., that mixing bowls are big enough for little hands to move a spoon in). Cookie sheets, a good frying pan, and a blender are important to have on hand, too. There are several tools that I use in the recipes that are excellent for giving your child sensory input, for example, a garlic press and a juicer to squeeze lemons. If you don't already own those tools, they are really worth investing in! Check out the cookware section on my blog (*www.kitchenclassroom4kids.com*) to find really reasonably priced kitchen tools. There are other items that you may or may not want to purchase: I love having different size muffin tins on hand, for example, but you can always set muffin papers on a cookie sheet and make muffins that way. Write to me with any cookware questions at Gabrielle@kitchenclassroom4kids.com and I'll try to help you think creatively about your needs!

- *How should I choose a good recipe to start with?* I've organized the recipes in each section by level of difficulty, starting with the easiest. If cooking is a new activity for you and your child, steer her toward one of the simple recipes like "Fruit Salad" or "Bugs on a Log." Look at the color photos of the finished concoctions and let your child help choose one.

    In addition, you'll notice that each recipe has a symbol next to it. Each symbol corresponds with a particular academic area or skill set. If your child is particularly "rammy" on a given day, you might choose a recipe that involves lots of sensory input. If you're working on literacy skills with your child, you might opt for a recipe that highlights those skills.

- *Do I have the basics in my pantry?* For me, whether you are cooking GFCF or not, there are a few essential items to always keep in stock: olive oil, sea salt, honey, lemons, garlic, frozen organic chicken breasts, eggs, and potatoes. Beside fresh fruits and vegetables, which I also always have on hand, these items will allow you to cook up a quick, healthy meal any time. If you are just starting out the GFCF diet, take a look at the Resource section of this book for helpful online articles about what items to keep in your pantry. If you look at your pantry and realize that you need to make a shopping trip before you start cooking, see the next section and consider how shopping can be an educational, experience-sharing opportunity for you and your child.

- *Do I have all of the ingredients in the house or do I need to take a shopping trip?*
    - For a first cooking experience, you'll want to have all of the ingredients set out and ready to go.
    - Make sure you have extra of everything and make sure that tops and lids are fastened securely. When George and

I first started cooking together, he was in a dumping phase, and a bag of flour could be poured on the floor if I left our cooking area for a moment. (Luckily, we've come a long way since that phase!)

- It makes sense to put a reasonable amount of frequently used ingredients, like salt, baking powder, and cinnamon, into small plastic, resealable containers with lids so if spills happen you don't lose all of your ingredients.
- As children develop in cognition and in comfort in the kitchen, gathering ingredients for a recipe can be part of your shared experience. You can look together for items in your spice rack, pantry, in the fridge, etc.
- Eventually, you might make shopping at the supermarket with your child part of the whole cooking experience. This is a fantastic opportunity to practice reading, math, and motor skills! (More on this later.)

- *What will my child's role be in the cooking activity?* Start small. You may begin with having the fruit in "Fruit salad" already chopped, for example, and have your child simply toss the pieces into the bowl and then mix it with a spoon. Observe your child as you work and notice what tasks seem easy and what tasks are more difficult. Ask an older sibling, friend, or parent to photograph or videotape your child or student cooking. Later you can look at these with an eye for what is working during the cooking process and what needs to be tweaked. (Undoubtedly, your child will enjoy and learn from the experience of watching himself star in his own cooking video!) As your child's skills develop, you can add more steps for him to do.

- *Where will my child sit/stand for the activity?* Is your child tall enough to reach your kitchen counter or will she need a stool or small chair? Is sitting together at a table a more effective way to focus your child's attention? You may need to experiment with sitting vs. standing for cooking. When June was small (eighteen to twenty months), she would sometimes sit right on the kitchen counter, while George stood on a small stool at the counter and I stood in between them.

- *How am I going to deal with the mess of it all?* First, I recommend accepting that making a mess while cooking is inevitable, especially at first. My attitude is that messes can always be cleaned up. I am concerned when I see some parents or teachers feeling so anxious about making a mess that children become inhibited or pick up and internalize an anxious energy. That is not healthy for anyone, especially for a child who is prone to anxiety. With some simple framing, you can reduce messes and focus on sharing experience with your child. For example:

- Put plastic tablecloths or newspaper down on the floor under you and on your work surface that can be easily picked up and shaken outside or trashed if too messy.
- If I am not working by my sink, I keep a large dishpan nearby so that I can stick dirty bowls, spoons, and containers right into it.
- Likewise, if you're not near your kitchen garbage can or compost, keep a large bowl nearby for dumping things such as eggshells, fruit peels, and pits, etc.
- Put your kids to work! As children develop, they can become active participants in the clean-up process. Believe it or not, cleaning up can be just as fun and educational (while providing sensory input) as cooking. (More on this in the section called Developing Gross Motor Skills in Chapter 4.)

Framing Your Shopping Experience

When George was a toddler, before we had any inclination that his development was not typical, we *did* know that he was an unusually active little boy, which meant that he ran a lot and we chased a lot. When I had to do something like go to the grocery store, for example, I counted on a sugary snack to keep George entertained in the front of the cart while I dashed around the store like a madwoman trying to grab everything that I needed before he finished his giant size M&M cookie and morphed into a truly wild child. When I was generally about two-thirds of the way through the grocery list, he would start shrieking at the top of his lungs until I let him out of the cart and then—you guessed it—he would run and I would chase. I've kind of repressed the memories of actually going through the check-out line and paying for my groceries, but I vaguely remember that more sugar was involved, followed by a shrieking car ride home. Good times.

I now have enough distance from those times to be able to look back and have compassion for both George and myself…and the store clerks and cashiers who helped us…and the old women who gave me looks of steel. I can even laugh a little about what disasters those shopping trips were. When George was four years old and we began RDI, I learned how I could take ordinary life moments, like going shopping, and turn them into opportunities for connection and learning. As I got better able to frame our shopping experiences and George's cognitive, emotional, and social abilities began to grow, shopping became fun for us. It is now one of our favorite activities to do together and that little toddler who ran from me shrieking is now a really big helper throughout the shopping process!

The following are suggestions for framing a positive shopping experience:

- *Prepare a list together before you go.* Look at a recipe together and say out loud the items that you need to shop for. Sound out the words aloud as you write the ingredients down. You might also create a reproducible master list that includes essentially any and all items (in alphabetical order) that you might purchase at the store. Run down the list with your child and highlight all the items you'll need to purchase for a particular recipe. For older children who are writing or starting to write, making up a list and categorizing the foods by themselves is great practice. If your child prefers pictures, you could make a list with pictures of what you plan to buy. Cut out labels from discarded food boxes or supermarket circulars, or go to Google images or a site with free clipart or images (see the Resource section for ideas) and look up pictures together; print them out, cut them, and glue them onto a clean piece of paper. Making up a shopping list could be a morning-long activity—full of literacy and fine motor practice as well as sensory input

- *Give your child a clearly defined role* at the store. For George, who needs some help grounding his body in space, pushing the shopping cart is very centering. When he was younger, I needed to pull and steer the front of it, but now he can maneuver the cart on his own. It also allows him to focus and pay attention to people around him. Another role that both of my kids play is being the shopper. I will name an item on the list for them to look for. I may point out a picture of apples and June will go find the apples. I will tell George that we need six apples, and he will count them as we put them in the bag. The more active a role that the kids can play, the more engaged (and less whiny!) they are during our shopping experience.

- *Use patterns to create co-regulation.* Co-regulation is term used in RDI that refers to children taking their share of responsibility and interest in reciprocal interaction. Patterns can help children with this process. They are a means by which children can process information and make sense of the world around them. Repeating any action—putting apples in a bag, for example—gives the child a chance to practice and internalize a process. I use patterns frequently when shopping with George. Rather than telling George a directive like, "Put the food on the checkout conveyer belt," I will create a pattern that engages him in the action. It might be me taking an item from the cart and handing it to him to put on the conveyer belt, or it might be me gesturing to him to take an item from the cart and hand it to me, who puts it on the checkout conveyer belt. As we get the pattern started, he is able to follow and complete the work of unloading the cart with me. There are lots of patterns that can be established throughout your shopping trip: filling bags with produce, lifting water bottles, etc. Think about how many patterns you can create during your shopping experience.

- *Shop when neither of you is hungry.* This is common sense advice but I have found that our blood sugar levels have a huge impact on how successful our shopping trip is! If George is hungry, he'll just want to eat a treat that we select rather than help me out. And if I'm hungry, I'm a very cranky mom.

- *Shop at times when the store is not busy and crowded.* Any child (or adult!) can feel overwhelmed in an overcrowded store, and so much more so for a child who has sensory processing issues and communication struggles. Get to know the busy and slow times at your local stores and plan your shopping trips accordingly. We all have times when we just can't make that happen but it's a good goal. I ended up picking up some last minute items at my local Whole Foods store with both kids in tow the Wednesday before last Thanksgiving, when the store was a madhouse. I was amazed at how calm and regulated both kids were able to stay as we navigated very crowded aisles and stood in a very long check-out line. It was clear that they had internalized our shopping process and were able to adjust and generalize their earlier, calm experiences to this one.

- *Know your child's attention span and adjust your schedule accordingly.* If you aren't used to shopping with your child or shopping in this kind of way, start with a short list. Pick up half a dozen items and get out of there! As your shopping experiences grow more successful for you and your child, build up your lists and the time that you spend at the store. I know this means that you might need to come back to the store on your own (I used to do this a lot when my husband got home from work and my kids were asleep), but it may be worth it so that you can help your child build up his tolerance and enjoyment of shopping.

- *Make a pleasurable moment* happen when you shop. If your store has a café area, stop and have a piece of fruit or snack together. When we shop at our local Trader Joe's, my children look forward to getting balloons and stickers from the checkout clerk. These little moments are wonderful incentives for making the whole experience a pleasant one for all of us. For some children, a treat at the end of the shopping trip is a nice reward. For others, a little treat at the beginning of the shopping trip can be motivating.

- *Bring a special toy along* because you never know when the store might be extra crowded, your kid might suddenly become bored, or the whole thing just stops working for some mysterious reason. I always carry a couple of special "store" toys in the car or my purse that the kids can only play with during these times.

- *Get to know some clerks* at your local stores, especially if you are going to go slow and work with your child as you checkout. I have found that most clerks are supportive and encouraging of my process with George. Clearly a friendly smile and some conversation makes them feel connected to us and what we are doing (and probably breaks up the monotony of their work day). I have even taken pictures of different clerks (with permission, of course!) for books that I have made George about shopping—and the clerks always get excited to be featured in our books. I have never stopped to explain that my child has autism and that I am using shopping as a means for him to learn; the clerks just seem to "get" what I'm doing. Now George is just a big helper and we move through the line as quickly as anyone. I'm an "It Takes a Village" kind of person in terms of my outlook on life and I enlist everyone that I can to help me remediate my child's autism. It's worth the effort to find those kind, friendly clerks and avoid any that give off bad vibes!

- *Keep the work going when you get home.* Getting the groceries out of the car and put away is an awesome opportunity for heavy lifting (sensory input)! Start with a bag that your child can handle. She may be able to lift it or may need to drag it. Putting away the groceries is also an excellent opportunity for language and communication. You can label items and categorize them too: fresh vegetables go here; canned vegetables go there, etc.

Chapter 4
Cooking and Child Development

As you frame your cooking experience, it is important to consider your child's fine motor, gross motor, and cognitive development—where your child is now developmentally and where you'd ideally like him to be. Throughout this introductory material and in the actual *The Kitchen Classroom* recipes you'll find numerous ideas to encourage your child to stretch his abilities in ways that are meaningful and fun. As his skills develop, your child's attention to the cooking process will grow, too.

One of the most exciting aspects of cooking with my children is watching them take on more of the actions of a given recipe as they hone their skills over time. When June was about twenty months old, she would often hang out in the kitchen when George and I were cooking and would want to take a turn stirring with him. Once she had her turn, her attention turned away from cooking, and that was fine. June is a very musical child and was happy to bang on pots and pans with different utensils, creating a unique symphony, while George, then four-and-a-half, measured, mashed, and mixed our ingredients. As June's fine motor skills began to develop more, I would offer her other ways of getting involved in our cooking work: tearing lettuce leaves, breaking celery stalks, pounding down cookie or pizza dough. Between ages two and three, June's skills developed to the point where she could—and wanted to be—an equal partner with George and me and we began to work together more often as a threesome.

The recipes in *The Kitchen Classroom* are best suited for toddlers, preschoolers, and elementary school age children, and you will want to use them in the way that is most appropriate for where your child is developmentally. (But I have many grown-up friends who didn't previously cook and appreciate the step-by-step manner of these recipes and are using them to start cooking!) In terms of children, a typically developing six-year-old, for example, may be able to read through all of the directions with you and follow all of the steps in the "Mickey Pancakes" recipe, while a three-year-old may be able to pour and stir the ingredients but may have less interest in watching you cook and flip the pancakes. It will take some trial and error to discover exactly how much cooking work is right for your child, and even then, her attention will vary based on the time of day, how tired she is, competing interests, etc. If a recipe doesn't work optimally one day, don't give up—it may come together easily the second time that you try it.

Developing Fine Motor Skills

The fine motor skills that are automatic to us as adults require practice for young children. Manipulating fingers accurately requires a balance of muscle tone, strength, and hand stability. When George was first undergoing evaluations for developmental delays, I learned about the importance of fine motor control for children. A number of occupational therapists pointed out his problems doing some basic skills—like gripping a crayon correctly—that children need to develop in order to eventually write and become independent in self-help skills like dressing. George's fine motor skills, between ages three and four, like many children who are on the autism spectrum, were clearly delayed.

Once I understood what kind of practice he would need to develop better fine motor control, we began working on those skills. One of the occupational therapists who worked with George introduced modified scissors, which bounced back open once he cut with them. George loved cutting paper and clearly received essential sensory input from this activity.

One afternoon around this time, I was preparing dinner and got out my little kitchen shears to cut up some fresh basil for a pesto sauce. George was sitting at a table in our kitchen, practicing cutting with some scrap paper. (By this time, George had moved from the assisted scissors to regular children's scissors.) I invited him over to the sink and helped him to hold the kitchen shears. With some assistance, I helped him to snip the freshly washed basil into pieces. He loved snipping them into the colander! Then we dried them with a kitchen towel and he stood on his little chair watching me put them in the chopper, along with pine nuts, olive oil, garlic, and salt to make a (dairy-free) sauce. This was one of the first moments I became aware of how cooking could be great practice for George's fine motor development, while giving him a sense of purpose. I mean, how much paper can a child stand to snip?

Below is a list of fine motor activities that you can work on with your child, using the recipes in *The Kitchen Classroom*. I recommend beginning with the activities at the top of the list, which require less fine motor control, and gradually working your way towards the items at the bottom of the list, which are more doable for children who have greater hand stability and more developed muscle tone.

Keep in mind that each child is unique in his development. Especially if your child has an autism diagnosis, he may be more fully developed in one set of skills than in another. Talk with your occupational therapist about which skills feel right for your child to practice. And, of course, keep the activity short in length and positive in tone. If your child tries tearing lettuce, but it is too difficult and frustrating, there is no failure; just something to return to another time when his skills are more developed.

Activities to develop fine motor skills include:

- Playing with utensils: put pots and pans and wooden spoons on the floor for banging or open the Tupperware drawer and let your child stack and nest containers
- Wiping down tables and counters
- Pushing the buttons on a food processor or blender
- Washing fruits and vegetables
- Kneading/pounding dough
- Pouring ingredients into a bowl
- Stirring with a big spoon
- Snapping green beans
- Breaking celery stalks or cauliflower
- Tearing lettuce or other greens
- Using a pincer grasp to pick up raisins or chocolate chips one at a time for decorating "Bugs on a Log" or cookies
- Squeezing lemons, limes, and oranges
- Spreading soft items (hummus, creamy almond butter, etc.) on crackers or bread
- Cutting with cookie cutters
- Cracking eggs and removing the shells
- Mashing with a fork
- Using a spatula to remove cookies from a cookie sheet
- Unscrewing lids and opening containers
- Cutting with kitchen shears
- Using an old-fashioned egg beater
- Cutting with a plastic, serrated knife (try using adult support first)
- Husking corn

Developing Gross Motor Skills

Gross motor skills involve large muscle groups and whole body movement. There are plenty of ways for kids to practice these skills in the kitchen—both when they are cooking and doing daily kitchen chores. Many children who have autism and other disabilities struggle with the motor planning required for effective large muscle movement; however, simple daily tasks, like carrying dishes to set the table for meals, are a great way to practice gross motor skills. For example, my son has greatly improved the core muscle strength in his trunk, which is required for successful posture in sitting, by helping me reach up for ingredients on our pantry shelves. If your child receives physical therapy to improve gross motor skills, talk with your therapist about which of the following activities might be effective activities to work on with your child:

- Carrying grocery bags from the car into the home
- Carrying trash bags outside to cans
- Unpacking and shelving cans and boxes of food
- Lifting and carrying cookie sheets from counter to oven
- Taking dirty dishes to the sink
- Pushing chairs under the table after meals
- Loading and unloading the dishwasher
- Taking out and putting away pots and pans
- Carrying a stack of dishes to the table and setting the table
- Pushing a wet mop over the kitchen floor
- Holding a bowl under one arm and stirring thick batter with a spoon with the other
- Kneading/pounding dough
- Shaking liquids in a sealed container
- Sweeping with a broom
- Mopping up spills from the floor on hands and knees with a wet rag

Developing Cognitive Skills

The kitchen is a wonderful place to work on your child's cognitive abilities; so much language and math learning naturally takes place each time that you cook together. Below are some of the ways that I highlight speech and language, literacy, math, and science skills when I am cooking with my children and my students. You don't need to emphasize all of these different learning areas each time that you cook—that could turn a fifteen-minute activity into an hour-long experience— which may exceed your children's attention span. But as you work together, even on a short activity, take moments to highlight language learning and moments to highlight math skills.

Literacy

Because the directions for the recipes on *The Kitchen Classroom* CD-ROM are written out with words *and* illustrated with photos, children who are visual learners have an opportunity to "read" in images. When it's cooking time, George and I pull out the binder of recipes that I've created (printed out from the CD-ROM) and sit down at the table where we often read books together. I point to the words while I'm reading, which gives George practice in visual scanning from left to right and in moving down the lines. We look at the pictures in the recipe and I ask him to point to the pictures as I read the words. George is minimally verbal and his speech is really just emerging, but he has a lot of receptive language and I know how important it is to develop pre-reading skills. He knows most of his letters so we sometimes play little games to identify letters. For example, he'll find the picture of an egg and I'll say something like "Egg starts with 'E.' Can you find the 'E?'"

It's a good practice to read through a recipe with your kids an hour or two in advance of cooking. Read it together like a story. In many ways, recipes are like stories in that they contain a beginning, middle, and an end. Sequencing is a basic literacy skill and it helps your child learn to follow the order of events in a story. I find that if we look at the recipe together first and then come back to it a few hours later, my kids will recall some of the ingredients and steps. If your child is very young or is not very interested in books and reading yet, do a short "skim through" of the recipe, just highlighting a few pictures. My experience is that each time you return to the recipe, she will become more interested in looking at the pictures, letters, and words.

After reviewing the recipe, go gather your ingredients together. Carry over the pre-reading lesson by pointing out letters on packages. "Oh look, here is the 'E' for 'egg' right here on the egg carton!" If your child is already reading, encourage him to read labels, package contents, etc. as you gather ingredients.

A good way to introduce language and pre-reading opportunities and reinforce acquired vocabulary to the cooking experience is to actually label things all over your kitchen, including in your pantry, refrigerator, and freezer (use freezer tape). Post printed words along with free clipart symbols, photographs, sign language signs, picture exchange communication system symbols (PECS), poison notices, etc.

Other activities to develop literacy skills include:

- Sorting foods by colors, shape, and size
- Learning letters by making their shapes out of food (use letter shaped cookie cutters or just mold letters out of cookie dough)
- Practicing left/right orientation by asking your child to put the egg-shells to the left of the bowl or hand you the spoon to her right
- Asking open-ended questions throughout the cooking experience, such as "What do you think will happen when we put this in the oven?"
- Labeling sensory experiences, e.g., "This dough sure is sticky" or "Those apples are very hot!"
- Shopping in the supermarket or in your own kitchen; making up lists and going hunting for words on labels that match your list

George is not reading yet, but he is showing an emerging interest in letters and pictures and how they are all connected. By practicing turn-taking, integrating sensory experiences with language, creating a visually stimulating experience, and increasing attention, we are creating an environment in the kitchen that fosters literacy. I believe that George is getting closer to making the cognitive leap to combining letters into words and I am confident that our time "reading" in the kitchen is helping to build that foundation.

Speech and Language

Because my son struggles with speech and language, I have worked to find a variety of ways to help him acquire these important communication tools. Cooking has been an incredible, natural way of expanding his vocabulary, both expressively and receptively. Think of all the words that are related to cooking, including:

- Verbs like stir, pour, shake, cut, pound, wash
- Nouns like names of fruits, vegetables, pantry items, spices, appliances, cookware
- Adjectives to describe smells (sweet, acidic, buttery), tastes (salty, sour, spicy), and textures (gooey, sticky, smooth)
- Prepositions like *in* the bowl, *on* the counter, *after* the dry ingredients go in

In my experience, using *less* verbal language as we cook, rather than bombarding George with words, helps his auditory processing skills. As we stir batter together, I may start a rhythmic chant: *stirring, stirring, stirring…*and then pause. It is extremely gratifying when George looks up at me and says, "Stirring!" or when he remembers a phrase that we have used in the kitchen before and relates it spontaneously to an action.

One of the fun activities that I've used to reinforce vocabulary that George already knows is to go on a little treasure hunt to find our ingredients. This works particularly well if you've labeled items in your kitchen. "Hmm…where could the flour be?" We open cupboards and canisters until George correctly locates the flour. "There it is! You found the flour!"

Math

I am not, have never been, and probably will never be a "math person," but I appreciate the need for mathematical accuracy when it comes to cooking and baking. For children, recipes are a natural place to begin connecting numbers and counting to something concrete and tangible.

Start with **counting**, even if your child is not counting yet. Wash strawberries for "Fruit Salad" and count out a dozen. Place a strawberry in your child's hand each time you say a number. Put them in a bowl and practice counting them again. Anything in your recipe can be counted: the number of cookies or pancakes that you make; the number of "bugs" you put on your almond butter logs; the number of tomatoes that you toss into your salad. You can also work on number skills when you set the oven **temperature** and the kitchen timer.

Cooking is also a great opportunity to **measure**…everything. Start by discussing the mathematical concept of "**more**" and "**less**." As you measure out your ingredients, take note of whether you are using more baking soda or more flour; less cinnamon or less nutmeg. Ask your child to add "more" flour to the bowl; one "more" egg; pour some water out of the bowl so there is "less."

Teach **relative sizes**, e.g., "Hand me the *biggest* measuring cup" or "This bowl is too *little*. Get me the *next biggest* one." Then move on to **fractions**. Talk about serving/portion sizes (pieces, slices). How many slices do we need to make in the "Pizza Pie" so everyone in our family gets two slices? How many cookies can each of your friends eat from the ten that are on the cooling rack? What is the appropriate amount of food to eat to get fueled up without getting overstuffed?

Practice **grouping** and **sorting** food and kitchen utensils with your child. Match up objects that have traits in common, such as size, shape, and other features. For example, when making "Build-Your-Own Veggie Skewers," talk about which vegetables are green or long and skinny. Use descriptors and this becomes an opportunity for learning about **topics/categories**, which is a communication skill. When it's time to empty the dishwasher, have your child sort the clean silverware as he puts it away in the drawer.

Make **patterns** and sequences with food, i.e., toss a strawberry into the bowl when making "Fruit Salad" and then a banana coin, strawberry, then banana. Ask your child what comes next. Make a repeating pattern out of the toppings on your "Pizza Pie." Help your child count out the number of plates, spoons, forks, etc. (one-to-one correspondence) and follow the correct pattern to set the table.

Sequencing, when it comes to following directions in a recipe, is also an important skill to develop for math. When you read through a recipe, point out its sequence. Ask your child to predict what would happen if you did the second step before the first. Predicting and **estimating** are important math concepts as well. Ask your child to guess how long the cookies will take to bake. Then set kitchen **timer** and look at the **clock** to determine when they'll be ready to eat. There's nothing like the promise of fresh baked goods to entice a child to learn to tell time.

As children acquire more math skills, you can give them bigger challenges. How many half cups does it take to make a whole cup? How many one-third cups? Take out empty measuring cups and **compare** their sizes.

Science

Cooking is essentially chemistry, so conjure up your child's inner scientist and encourage her creativity in the kitchen. There are many opportunities for short science lessons as you cook. For example, many of the recipes in *The Kitchen Classroom* include combining wet and dry ingredients. You can take a moment to ask your child what she thinks will happen when you pour the wet stuff into the dry stuff. Putting a question like that out to your child encourages her ability to form a hypothesis. If your child doesn't have the verbal skills to respond to a question like that, it doesn't mean that she isn't taking in the question. Pause after you combine wet and dry ingredients and spotlight what has happened: "Oh wow—it has become a wet and sticky dough now!"

Or discuss what happens to the flavor, color, and smell of your "Fruity Smoothie" when you experiment with adding in different kinds of fruits. What if you use ¾ fruit in the smoothie and ¼ vegetables (scandalous, I know!)? Can your child taste the vegetable?

Watching water change forms—from freezing into ice cubes to boiling on the stovetop—is another very interesting scientific process that you can observe in the kitchen. Children can practice filling ice cube trays with water using a small measuring cup. (You'll need ice cubes for our "Lemonade" recipe.) Put the trays in the freezer and set the timer for an hour, then go check whether they've frozen yet. Record how long it takes for the water to change form from liquid to solid. (We have fun making juice cubes to use in smoothies or other iced drinks.) It's also interesting to note how water can evaporate as you cook. Making rice, for example, is an opportunity to spotlight how the water you poured into the pan disappears when the rice is fully cooked.

Cooking in the oven is an ideal time to talk about the concept of temperature—especially since we want to emphasize that when we turn on the oven, it gets hot! Talk about the different means we use to cook our food—from a toaster, to a stovetop, to an oven. This is a good time to reinforce safety rules about never touching the hot oven or stovetop.

Cooking in the Classroom

If you will be cooking with a classroom of children, it's likely they will vary in terms of their developmental levels and skills. Start by gathering the students together for circle time, introduce the recipe with the class as a whole, and read it together as a story. Point to the photos as you read and stop along the way to ask open-ended questions.

One way to create an optimum experience for all of the children is to have each cooking activity set up as a station, where two to four children can work together with an adult, so that each child can take on a role in the recipe and be an active participant. As a teacher, you may choose to emphasize language, math, science, or pre-reading skills within the recipe.

Just as with cooking in the home, anticipate that some mess will be involved; so help your students learn to be part of the clean-up process. And, if you are able, take some digital photos to share with parents, who will be impressed to see what their children are doing in your classroom and may become inspired to cook with their child at home!

Chapter 5
Cooking and Sensory Input

Young children learn about the world through their senses of smell, taste, touch, hearing, and seeing. The kitchen offers so many opportunities to encourage sensory exploration: comparing the smells of sweet and savory spices; tasting bites of cookies from the oven; feeling the sensation of fresh dough in the palm of your hand; listening for the whistle of the tea kettle or the popping of corn; seeing how a smooth batter rises into a cake. Each time you invite your child into a cooking experience, his world opens up in new ways.

Too often, young children spend much of their time in front of the television or computer where experiential learning is limited. Cooking with young children is an open-ended sensory experience that can lay a foundation for all kinds of cognitive learning as they grow. Once a child is able to differentiate between spices, for example, you can introduce the concept that different cultures favor different spices. As children begin to understand how geography, climate, economy, religion, and other factors influence a region's cuisine, they begin to perceive a multi-cultural world.

Cooking and Sensory Processing Disorder (SPD)

Most children on the autism spectrum experience SPD or some degree of difficulty with sensory processing, and many children who are not diagnosed with autism also have SPD. This means that they may perceive sensory information differently from a neurotypical child. Their processing difficulties may relate to the tactile sense (touching); vestibular sense (relating to balance); proprioceptive sense (relating to movement, body control, and motor planning); or any combination of these. Many children—not only those with autism and other special needs—have textural food sensitivities. A benefit of cooking and eating with your children is that you're developing their palates! Kids are far more likely to eat—or at least try—a dish that they've helped prepare. Getting creative with food presentation (see the "Bugs on a Log" or "Funny Face Toast" recipes) might also encourage your children to be more adventurous in the dining room.

A thorough evaluation from an occupational therapist who specializes in sensory integration can help you identify which areas are challenges for your child and how you can create activities to help her. If your child has serious eating issues, always consult an expert before embarking on any special diets or feeding techniques.

Sensory Seeking

Many therapists and teachers who have worked with George have described him as a "sensory seeker," meaning he craves sensory information, especially in the form of touch and smell. Often, if we are going somewhere that will require him to sit for more than twenty minutes (a long car ride, a family gathering, a music concert), I will take sensory putty along for him to squeeze, which relaxes his body and allows him to focus on what is happening around him.

When I started cooking with George, I realized that there are many opportunities for him to get the sensory input that he seeks during our activities. One of the first suggestions that Jennifer Paget, our RDI consultant, gave me was to have George crack eggs. At the time, I thought this was a completely crazy idea! Because of how out of whack George's overall vestibular system was at the time, he often moved through a room like a bull in a china shop. I knew that George didn't have the fine motor control needed to carefully crack an egg and not drip it everywhere. I imagined egg all over my kitchen floor, splattered on the ceiling, dripping all over George's clothes…you get the idea. But because I trusted Jennifer's insights about George, I listened to her plan.

She demonstrated with George. She took out two bowls. In the first, she put an egg, and then smashed it into the bottom of the bowl. She pulled out the broken shell, letting the egg drip out and tossed the broken shell into the other bowl. Then she handed George an egg and he did the same thing. Smash egg in the bowl; put eggshell neatly in the other bowl.

Not only was the egg cracked and ready to use in cookie dough, George clearly loved the experience of cracking it. I am sure the sensory experience of cracking eggs was one of the "hooks" that got him engaged in cooking. The smashing of the egg into the bottom of the bowl gave his sensory seeking system some satisfying input. Now he sometimes takes a moment and crackles the broken eggshells in the bowl, because that is more tactile input, although lately he is more interested in moving forward in the recipe than having a "sensory seeking moment."

If your child craves tactile sensory input, think of the many ways he can experience it while cooking:

- Cracking eggs
- Pounding dough
- Smashing cookies for pie crusts
- Rolling cookie dough in hands
- Rolling out "snakes" with (GF) pretzel dough
- Tearing lettuce and other vegetables
- Washing fruit, vegetables, and dirty dishes
- Chopping with a plastic, serrated knife
- Mincing garlic
- Using a mortar and pestle
- Stirring heavy dough
- Sprinkling toppings
- Squeezing oranges and lemons for juice
- …the list goes on!

If your child is a "sensory seeker," there is always a chance that a little more mess may be involved. Again, the more that you can plan ahead, the easier your clean up will be. Because George loves the sensation of water on his hands, he is happy to stand at the sink and rinse out our cooking bowls. He is starting to do a good, thorough job of washing out bowls with a sponge. Seeking out tactile sensation can have its advantages when used in appropriate ways!

Sensory Avoidance

Some children react to sensation with avoidance or resistance. They may feel great discomfort when "messy things" touch their skin. For these "sensory avoiders," cooking activities might seem daunting at first, but ultimately offer great opportunities for desensitization and learning. Cooking offers a safe, structured way to experience different sensory input.

If this profile sounds like your child, begin slowly with your cooking activities. She may feel most comfortable pouring dry ingredients in a bowl, rather than dealing with sticky, gooey dough once liquid ingredients are added. Perhaps her role is to dump in flour and baking soda and mix it up, while you add the eggs and honey. Maybe she will just watch you mix the wet dough at first. Show how safe it is to use a spoon or other utensil to create some distance from the dough.

If your child is extremely tactilely defensive you can provide him with clean latex gloves, but cooking on a regular basis will likely increase his tolerance for textures. You may be surprised when working on the same recipe for the third time, your child begins to show an interest in the "wet stuff." After he feels comfortable mixing with a long spoon, you can introduce recipes that require rolling in the hand, like "Carob-

Coconut Cookies." If your child rolls one or two cookies, celebrate big, and emphasize what a great job he has done.

Cookie cutters are another fun way to get children with tactile defensiveness working with dough. The recipe for "Apple Hamantashen" makes a nice dough that is easy to use with cookie cutters. Look in kitchen stores or even dollar stores for cookie cutters with special themes that will interest your child.

Auditory Defensiveness (or It's Too Loud!)

Children with sensory integration disorder may have extra sensitivity to loud noises. Certain kitchen tools—a hand mixer, blender, or even the dishwasher—may sound extraordinarily harsh to their ears and may set off a fear/anxiety reaction. If your child tends to startle with loud or sudden noises, take precautions before using any kitchen tool that makes a loud sound. When my son and I first began making smoothies in the blender, I would pause before turning the blender on, cover my ears, and say, "Loud." George would go into another room while I turned the blender on. Other ideas to decrease your child's sensitivity to noise include:

- providing your child with soft ear plugs or a fabric headband that may help muffle or dampen sounds
- providing deep pressure in the form of hugs or hand squeezes
- allowing your child to be the one in control of switching the blender or mixer on and off
- Providing some preparation time by counting to five before turning on the loud tool

Over time, George has become used to the sound of the blender and other kitchen tools and is able to tolerate them just fine. If you have any doubt that a sound may frighten your child, give a warning and help your child find a comfortable place far enough away from the sound that it won't distress her. I have also noted that my daughter, who has no sensory integration issues, can sometimes be scared of kitchen tools like the mixer and prefers being in another room when I'm using them.

Oral Defensiveness

Many children with sensory processing issues experience oral defensiveness, or food avoidance, which may be related to over-registration of tactile input to the mouth. These kids don't tolerate the normal variety of textures common in food. Some children may only want to eat things that make a crunch, while others will only tolerate totally smooth food. Oral defensiveness is a very serious issue because it can affect the nutritional value of what a child eats. Parents can get easily worn down by daily, ongoing struggles over food and may give up and simply allow their child to eat one or two food items repeatedly. If this situation resonates for you, it is important to find a physician or occupational therapist who can work with you and your child regarding his feeding issues.

Therapy designed to help a child overcome oral defensiveness is usually a very slow, gradual process. It often involves using a preferred food to entice the child to begin to tolerate minute pieces of texture (mixed in with the preferred taste) and gradually "working up" to more complex ones. Engaging the mouth in activities like chewing gum, crunching on crackers and carrot sticks, and sucking on popsicles or thickened liquid through a straw can help calm a child who is over-responsive to things in her mouth. But whether your child seeks or avoids stimulation to her mouth, because diet and nutrition is so important for a growing child, always consult your child's occupational therapist, speech and language therapist, and pediatrician on these matters.

As a young toddler, my son would eat (or at least try) everything—all fruits, avocados, smoked fish, hot dogs, puffed rice, yogurt, etc. But between the ages of two and three, he began eating fewer foods. I was told by many experienced parents that this stage is a normal developmental phase, but it concerned me. Between ages three and four, George ate only carbohydrates and some dairy—no proteins, no fruits, no vegetables. He wanted pretzels, fish crackers, pizza, bagels, etc. Many children with autism display food selectivity, and George fell into this camp. I was unbelievably concerned and began reading about children with autism who respond well to a gluten-free/casein-free diet (learn more about the diet in a later chapter). I decided to try it with George, following a gradual plan of taking out gluten and casein and introducing GFCF foods. Within a week of taking out some of the gluten in his diet, George began eating fruits. Then proteins. Then vegetables. He began to look healthier and his digestion greatly improved, as you can imagine.

The variety of foods that George eats now is wonderful. Still, he has some oral defensive issues and prefers foods that "crunch" above all others. Sometimes he is finicky about trying a new food and sometimes I can tell that if the look or smell of a favorite food is slightly off, he will reject it. He also goes through phases in which he will absolutely love a certain kind of food, say strawberries, and then wake up one day and reject them. He will usually come back to the food after a one to two month hiatus.

Even though George still definitely has his share of quirkiness around food, our cooking together, along with removing the gluten and casein from his diet, has had a tremendous influence on expanding the variety of foods that he will eat. If George has cooked something, he will most definitely try it. He may not finish it, he may not go for seconds, but he will generally try it. Hopefully, cooking with your child will likewise open up a world of new foods and optimal nutrition.

Chapter 6
Kitchen Safety

Above all else, it is critical for you, the adult, to create a safe working environment to cook in with your child. Especially if your child has difficulty with attention, focus, or language processing, it is imperative that you set up your cooking experiences so that your child will not get hurt. Review the following steps for proper planning and precautions:

1. **Wash hands with soap and warm water** before starting any recipe and frequently throughout, especially if you or your child has been handling raw fruit, vegetables, meat, eggs, or sneezes, wipes his nose, coughs, and so forth.

2. **Prevent food contamination and foodborne illness.** Hands, countertops, kitchen utensils (e.g., knives, cutting boards), and even already cooked foods can become contaminated with raw meat and eggs in any kitchen—particularly those with inexperienced cooks. Either have extra, unused utensils on hand or be sure to thoroughly wash with soap and hot water any tools you need to reuse. Take care to follow food safety guidelines when thawing frozen meats and be sure to cook meat and eggs fully and at the appropriate temperature. And don't forget to wash all fruits and vegetables well before eating them.

3. **Use the appropriate knife for your child.** This means that for all recipes with chopping, that you start by giving your child a butter knife or even a plastic knife. Teach your child appropriate knife skills, especially cutting away from your hands and body and away from

anyone near you. As she becomes competent at using that knife, you can introduce a knife with a sharper blade, but always stay close by your child if she is using a knife. It may be appropriate in some cases, for example, when chopping fresh herbs, to have your child use kitchen scissors. You may want to have your occupational therapist watch your child using a knife and recommend what size knife to use. Even as George gets more competent at cutting, I assist him hand over hand when using a blade that is sharper than a butter knife.

4. **Make the stove and burners "grown-up only" space.** Many of *The Kitchen Classroom* recipes require baking. Make taking pans, cookie sheets, etc. in and out of the oven a grown-up only job. Likewise, any part of a recipe that requires cooking on the stovetop should also be a grown-up only job. Point all pan handles away from the edge of the stove. To help your child to understand that a stovetop and oven can be hot and are not safe for a child to touch, you may want to use a picture symbol to help her learn to stay back. You can also do all of your cooking steps in an area of the kitchen away from the stove/oven to create some physical space as a barrier. A child-proof oven safety lock can also be used as a safeguard. I know some parents who have had success with putting down colored tape a foot or two from the stove and telling their kids they can't get any closer. I often place a small stool about two feet away from the stove so my children can remain a safe distance from the heat, but are still able to watch as I flip their pancakes.

5. **Only grown-ups should touch, carry, or cut hot foods or liquids.**

6. **Unplug small appliances** like toasters, blenders, coffee makers, and anything else that may be on your countertop near where you are working with your child. Unplugging them takes away the possibility of them being turned on accidentally.

7. **Have your child wear short sleeves or roll up long sleeves** so that clothing does not accidentally get caught in a mixer, toaster oven, etc. Long hair should also be pulled back into a ponytail.

8. **Have your child wear closed-toed shoes** in case a knife or heavy bowl gets knocked off the counter.

9. **Keep a fire extinguisher within your reach** and make sure that you know how to use it properly. Similarly, make sure that your fire and smoke alarms have new batteries in them and are working properly.

10. **Wipe up spills immediately** so that no one slips and falls.

11. **Make sure that if your child is working on a stool or small chair that it is at the right height** to reach the counter or table. Make sure that the stool or small chair is balanced evenly and doesn't wobble.

Chapter 7
Special Notes about the Gluten-Free/ Casein-Free Diet

Our Family's Story

Our family has tried a number of the recommended diets out there for children with autism. We started out on the GFCF diet, and then we spent a year on the Body Ecology Diet™, and a few months on the Specific Carbohydrate Diet™ before coming back to the GFCF diet. The other, more rigid programs did not yield any noticeable changes for our son, George.

Many parents who have children with autism spectrum disorder have found that the gluten-free/casein-free (GFCF) diet is helpful for their children in a variety of ways. There are also some parents who have expressed that the GFCF has played a role in "curing" their child's autism. I am <u>not</u> one of those parents. My son has been on the GFCF diet for about three years and is still clearly living with autism. That being said, we have discovered that there are wonderful benefits of the diet for George:

- He eats a wider variety of foods and has better nutrition on the diet.
- His digestive health (including regular bowel movements) is greatly improved on the diet.
- He sleeps better when on the diet.
- He is less hyperactive when on the diet.
- He has better emotional regulation (less frequent outbursts and melt-downs) when on the diet.

That is a pretty significant list in terms of George's ability to learn and our whole family's general health and well-being! Even if the only improvement that the diet yielded for us was George consistently sleeping through the night, I would be willing to do it. But seeing his digestive health improve and being a happier, more well-adjusted child on the diet is an incredible benefit, as well. That said, I have seen many, many children with autism who are doing wonderfully well with no dietary interventions. *Clearly, the GFCF diet does not have the same effect on every child with an ASD diagnosis.*

Although we initially removed all dairy products from George's diet, we were encouraged to reintroduce butter by the DAN ("Defeat Autism Now") doctor whom we first consulted about George's diet. Butter contains a very small amount of casein and we found that George could tolerate it well. I use organic butter in all of my cooking. If your child can't tolerate butter, I recommend using "Earth Balance" as an excellent replacement for butter. We have also begun re-introducing small amounts of other foods that contain casein (particularly hard cheeses, like cheddar) and have found that George tolerates them well. He currently eats regular cheese about three times a week and experiences no adverse effects. We have experimented with re-introducing gluten with disastrous results (crying jags, difficulty sleeping, hyperactivity, and other fun stuff). So though we allow for occasional gluten treats, we are committed to keeping gluten out of George's daily diet.

We also try to keep sugar and artificial ingredients down to a minimum. The recipes in *The Kitchen Classroom* use honey as a sweetener and you can experiment and cut down on the honey if it is too much for your child to tolerate. I know that some parents use agave or stevia (featured in the lemonade recipe) as sweeteners with great results.

How to Adapt Recipes in This Book

Since George now eats some dairy, most of the recipes in *The Kitchen Classroom* are written as GF recipes, but each of them can be adapted to suit your child's particular dietary needs. Unless your whole family is eating a GFCF diet, you'll need to pay close attention to avoid cross-contamination of gluten from kitchen tools, prep surfaces, and food products. If your child is on a fully gluten-free/casein-free diet, substitutions can be made with the many wonderful vegan products available these days. For butter, our family likes "Earth Balance." In place of milk, we prefer using almond milk or rice milk. There are a number of vegan cheeses on the market—you can compare brands and see which your prefer. If you would like to try a nondairy yogurt for your child, there are products on the market that are rice-based and some that are soy-based.

We use almond butter as the main nut butter in our home, but you could also try cashew or peanut butter. If your child has tree nut allergies, you can use soy butter in these recipes with wonderful results. The main flour that I use in baking is rice flour, but people who are on the Specific Carbohydrate Diet can modify these recipes using almond flour instead. If you are following the Body Ecology diet, you can modify these recipes by using quinoa (one of my family's favorite grains) in place of rice or noodles and quinoa flour in place of rice flour. I allow my children to eat a small amount of chocolate (not in the evenings!) but if you don't, try using carob chips in place of chocolate chips. I am happy to help you brainstorm about making substitutions in these recipes. In fact, if you have questions or ideas about substitutions, please drop me an email at Gabrielle@kitchenclassroom4kids.com and I will be happy to work with you!

You will notice that the recipes in *The Kitchen Classroom* have kid appeal but are also made of simple combinations of healthy, delicious ingredients that adults will absolutely appreciate. My cooking philosophy is all about simplicity: good ingredients with lots of flavor yield delicious results. As you and your child cook together more, you can increase your experimentation. Take one of my recipes and add almond or lemon extract rather than vanilla; compare the change in taste with your child. Try a spice like cardamom instead of cinnamon. Cooking is a wonderful way to help your child get to know his palate and to gradually open him up to the wide variety of spices, herbs, and flavors that make food so delicious!

Keeping Kosher

If your family follows the Jewish dietary laws known as *kashrut,* you will discover how uncomplicated it is to keep kosher while following the GFCF diet. The laws of kashrut require a separation of milk and meat products which can never be eaten together, so removing the dairy piece from your diet simplifies the coordination of meals. Of course, if you are using butter, any recipes with butter become "dairy," but if you choose to use a replacement like "Earth Balance," you will discover that most recipes in *The Kitchen Classroom* will work well with meat meals.

My Two Cents

There is *so* much pressure on us parents who have children with autism to "cure" our children with the right interventions, therapies, school, diet, and so on. The pressure can be truly maddening for us parents, as if we didn't face pressure enough! For me, it has been removing the expectation to "cure" my child that has allowed me to focus on being present for him to work on his neurological deficits while building our emotional relationship. My focus on the here and now—accepting where George is and what his challenges are—has allowed both of us to keep growing as individuals and building our connectedness. Striving towards a "cure" made me into a crazed, frantic parent, whereas working with RDI therapy and its focus on *remediation* has made me an aware, hopeful parent who duly notes both the challenge of parenting a child with autism and the wonderful rewards that come as a result of our ongoing work.

If you are a parent of a child with autism who has not yet tried dietary intervention, I urge you to give it a shot. What have you got to lose? (In the resource section of this book, you will find lots of websites that can help to get you started.) I hope that the interventions you attempt help your child as much as they have helped mine, but I encourage you to begin your explorations with realistic expectations. A diet may help your child, but "help" and "cure" are two very different things. If I had heard this kind of cautionary advice when starting my son out on the GFCF diet, perhaps it would have helped me avoid some of the heartbreak that I experienced when the diet didn't prove to be a "cure" as I had read it was for many other children.

All parents of children with autism want to find the best therapies for their children and we need to be united in supporting one another as we forge our individual journeys. I am discouraged when I read about and experience a division between parents who are doing dietary interventions and those who are not. Judgment is not going to help any of us; there is simply no one clear, cookie cutter path that works for every child with autism and I trust that every parent is doing his or her best.

My goal with *The Kitchen Classroom* is to provide a resource for you whether you are doing the GFCF diet or not. I wish to share my experiences in the hope that they will benefit others, just as so many helpful resources have helped my family. If diet is one part of your path, then I hope that these recipes will give you lots of creative inspiration and some really delicious meals! And if you're a parent of a child with autism but aren't using the GFCF diet for your child, please adapt these recipes, and use wheat products for goodness sake!

Symbol Key

 Math

 Science

 Literacy

 Communication/Language

 Social skills

 Sensory activity

 Fine motor

 Gross motor

"Crazy" Eggs

Mickey Pancakes

Funny Face Toast

Fruit Salad

Almond Butter Muffins

Better Than PB & J

Baked Apples

Chicken Wraps

Veggie Veggie Burgers

Sesame Salmon

Grilled "Cheese" Sandwich

Sweet Potato Latkes

Fried Rice & Veggies

Nut Butter Noodles

Chicken Sauté

Mama's Meatballs

Rice Noodle Lasagna

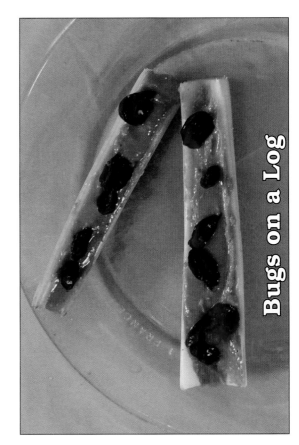

Pizza Pie

ABC Salad

Bugs on a Log

Favorite French Fries

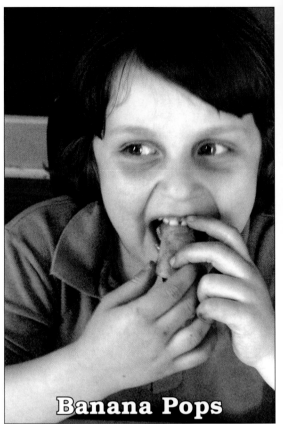

Banana Pops

Carrot Coins

Build-You-Own Veggie Skewers

Lemonade

Yummy Hummus

Tasty Trail Mix

Fruity Smoothies

Banana Chocolate Chip Bread

Apple Hamantashen

Crispy Rice Squares

Carob-Coconut Cookies

Funny Face Toast

Breakfast

"Crazy" Eggs

Fruit Salad

Mickey Pancakes

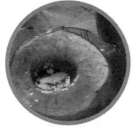

Baked Apples

Almond Butter Muffins

Funny Face Toast

Level I (easy)

Who says it's not okay to play with your food? Sometimes playing is just the thing your child needs. Kids with autism often have trouble interpreting facial expressions, and this is a great opportunity to practice making faces and reading them. Model a happy face for your child and have him try to reproduce it with fruit. Ask him to model a silly face for his sister and I'll bet she'll make one back at him.

Although George's fine motor skills make drawing with markers hard for him right now, he is able to practice his fine motor skills to create a representation of a face with this simple recipe that also makes a quick, nutritious breakfast. I usually prep the fruit ahead of time since mornings can be hectic, but as your child's fine motor and knife skills improve, he can help with this part.

Ingredients

GFCF bread
Nut butter (almond, peanut, etc.)
Dried fruit (e.g., raisins, cranberries, currants, cherries)
Fresh pre-cut fruit pieces (e.g., banana, apple, Clementine sections)

Tools

Plate
Cutting board
Sharp knife
Butter knife
Toaster

Directions

1. **Prepare the cooking area in advance. Clear all clutter. Pre-cut any fruit you think your child might select for his Funny Face Toast. Set out all ingredients and cooking utensils.**

2. **Read through the entire recipe and instructions (on the CD-ROM or print-outs) with your child, pointing to each word as you read.**

     Emphasize words that are specific to this recipe, like spread, push, dip, etc. Connect the words to the photos as you talk about what you'll be doing.

3. Wash hands.

 The sensation of the water will calm and ready your child for cooking. Take advantage of this time to do any last minute prep.

4. If your child likes his bread toasted, go ahead and toast it.

 Teach your child how to put the bread into the toaster and push down the plunger or turn the dial to turn it on. Be sure to stand close by.

5. When the bread is ready, put it on a plate and open your jar of nut butter.

   Let your child unscrew the jar, dip a knife in, and scoop out some nut butter. You may need to use hand over hand to help.

6. Demonstrate for your child how to spread the nut butter with the knife over the bread.

  Especially if this is a new skill, give encouragement and be patient. "Back and forth…back and forth…" works well. Use hand over hand if your child needs assistance.

7. Tell your child that it's time to make a "funny face."

 The first time you make a funny face, you can keep it simple and just use raisins. With George, I ask guided questions to help him with placement, such as "Where do the eyes go?" When he completes that step, I'll say, "Let's add a nose."

 As children get used to the idea of making a face on the bread, you can introduce more variations. Should we use a banana slice or an apple slice for the mouth? Work with your child step by step to put on eyes, a nose, mouth, and ears using the dried and fresh fruit. You might also add hair around the edges.

 Count how many grapes it takes to make eyes and how many raisins it takes to make a smiling mouth.

  You can make toast with different kinds of expressions and talk about what your toast is "feeling." We use a banana coin mouth to make a surprised face and an upside down apple slice to make a sad face. Depending on your child's developmental level, making Funny Face Toast can also be a good way to talk about how each of you is feeling that morning. If he's happy, he can make a happy face; if you're tired, you can make a tired-looking face, and so on.

"Crazy" Eggs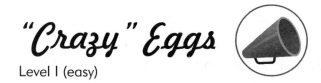

Level 1 (easy)

Between you and me, "Crazy" Eggs are just scrambled eggs with veggies snuck in there. But for my daughter, "Crazy" Eggs are an invitation to be creative. One morning, we were mixing up scrambled eggs together and I said, "Let's be crazy and put in some peppers!" June started laughing as I cooked an egg with leftover pieces of red pepper mixed in. When it was ready, she ate it right up. She wanted another egg, so I tried the same tact, "Let's be crazy and put in some carrots!" She laughed again and the rest is history. Since eggs require so little attention to prepare, they present a good opportunity to get some back and forth conversation going with my kids while we cook.

I usually prep the vegetables ahead of time since mornings can be hectic, but as your child's fine motor and knife skills improve, he can help with this part. Have a few choices of chopped vegetables on hand and let your child select from them. In time, he may choose three or four vegetables to add to the eggs. I figure that every bite of vegetable is adding nutrients into my children's diet, so start out small and hopefully you can add in more vegetables with time. Let the craziness begin!

Ingredients

Eggs (as many as you think you'll want)
Milk or milk substitute (e.g., almond, rice, or soy) (1 teaspoon for every egg)
¼ teaspoon salt
Pre-chopped vegetables (e.g., bell peppers, mushrooms, broccoli, carrot)
1 tablespoon butter or vegan butter substitute

Tools

Butter knife   Paper towel
Knife   Cutting board
Spatula   Medium-sized bowl
Whisk   Skillet
Measuring spoons

Directions

1. **Prepare the cooking area in advance. Clear all clutter. Pre-cut any vegetables you think your child might select for his "Crazy" Eggs. Set out all ingredients and cooking utensils.**

2. Read through the entire recipe and instructions (on the CD-ROM or print-outs) with your child, pointing to each word as you read.

Emphasize words that repeat, like whisk, pour, crack, etc. Connect the words to the photos as you talk about what you'll be doing.

3. Wash hands.

The sensation of the water will calm and ready your child for cooking. Take advantage of this time to do any last minute prep.

4. Crack egg(s) into a large bowl.

Have your child crack the eggs at the bottom of a medium-sized bowl. Let him punch them, stick his thumbs into them, etc. There is no wrong way to do this and he will choose the method that provides the type of sensory input he is seeking.

Have your child pick out the broken eggshell pieces and wipe them onto a paper towel. Then direct him to wash his hands. These activities provide excellent fine motor skill practice.

5. Add milk (or substitute) and salt to egg(s).

You can pre-pour the milk into a small container or pitcher that is easier for your child to handle.

Have your salt already poured into a small bowl so that your child can readily scoop it with a measuring spoon and level it off with a butter knife, which is great practice for fine motor skills.

6. Let your child choose some pieces of chopped vegetable and drop them into the egg mixture.

Picking up the small veggie pieces is great fine motor practice.

Because eggs cook so quickly, we usually make one at a time and try different vegetable combinations with each egg. Does your child have a favorite color? Point out the different colors of the vegetables and the color combinations you can create.

7. Use a whisk to stir briskly.

You can play a game of "Ready…set…stir!" and encourage your child to stir the egg mixture as fast as he can. If he is able to communicate verbally, you can take a turn stirring and he can take a turn saying "Ready…set…stir!"

8. Heat a skillet to medium and place butter in the pan.

  Situate your child a safe distance from the stovetop and watch together as the butter melts in the skillet. Talk about how it is changing forms.

9. When the butter melts, add egg and veggie mixture to the skillet and cook.

Using a spatula, push egg mixture to the center. Break apart large pieces of egg and then flip all of the egg over so that it cooks evenly. When nearly cooked through, consider adding in some shredded cheese or vegan cheese substitute for added protein.

10. Transfer eggs to a plate.

 Invite your child to blow on the eggs before eating them because they will be hot! Count to twenty together before taking the first bite.

 Comment on how delicious the "Crazy" Eggs look! Notice and talk about how the different vegetables taste. Which one is the sweetest? Which one is the crunchiest?

Fruit Salad

Level II (moderately difficult)

A great thing about fruit salad is that it can be a new and different mixture of fruit each time you make it. It's an ideal way to introduce categories, wherein different fruit can be sorted into different categories. You can practice sorting by color, shape, size, and so on. For children with autism, accepting variations can be difficult. If your child has one favorite fruit, he may always want that one fruit to be in the salad, but in time, you can experiment with interesting combinations.

These days I'm paying attention to what produce is seasonal and local. My family belongs to a CSA (community-supported agriculture) where produce from a local farmer is delivered to our neighborhood every week from April through November. We also shop at local farmers' markets together—another great opportunity to count, group, and sort!

Ingredients

A mixture of seasonal fruit combinations, such as:
- 2 bananas, 2 apples, 1 cup grapes
- 1 cup each fresh strawberries, blueberries, and raspberries
- 1 cup orange or Clementine sections, 2 pears, 1 cup pitted cherries
- 2 kiwis, 2 peaches, 1 cup melon

Tools

1 Large bowl	Cutting board
1 Serving bowl	Colander
Large spoon	Melon baller (optional)
Butter knife	

Directions

1. **Prepare the cooking area in advance. Clear all clutter. Set out all ingredients and cooking utensils.**

2. **Read through the entire recipe and instructions (on the CD-ROM or printouts) with your child, pointing to each word as you read.**

     Emphasize words that repeat, like cup, chop, mix, etc. Connect the words to the photos as you talk about what you'll be doing.

3. Wash hands.

The sensation of the water will calm and ready your child for cooking. Take advantage of this time to do any last minute prep.

4. Place any fruit that doesn't have a peel (grapes, peaches, berries, etc.) in a colander and run under cold water.

The sensation of the water will focus your child on the activity at hand.

Have your child turn the cold water on and count to ten out loud together while rinsing the fruit. Then have him turn off the faucet so as not to waste water.

5. Peel any fruit that has a "shell," take stems off, and divide oranges into sections.

You may need to start peeling the banana or orange yourself but then allow your child to finish on his own.

6. Using hand over hand with your child, slice fruit with a butter knife.

Start with soft fruit first (e.g., bananas), which are easiest to slice. If you're including melon in your salad, having your child use a melon baller to create bite-sized pieces is great fine motor practice.

7. Put all the fruit into a large bowl.

Create a pattern for your child to follow: grape, strawberry, banana...grape, strawberry, banana. Chant and repeat!

A few pieces may fly out of the bowl. If they do, react with a surprised face and pause. Point to the fruit pieces and allow your child to experience what in RDI we call "productive uncertainty." Maybe he will put the pieces back into the bowl; maybe, like George, he will notice them and eat them!

When all of your fruit is in the bowl, you can take a moment to count the different types together.

8. Encourage your child to spoon some fruit onto a plate.

Since fruit salad isn't hot or messy, it's the perfect dish for your child to practice serving with a large spoon. Enjoy!

Mickey Pancakes

Level II (moderately difficult)

When I was a kid and started making pancakes on my own (maybe I was eleven or twelve), I loved making pancakes in the shape of Mickey Mouse for my younger brother. When I started George on the GFCF diet, pancakes were the first recipe that I tried. Because George loves Mickey Mouse, I resurrected the Mickey pancake idea, and it was a hit! Mickey's shape is pretty easy to create with pancake batter, but if you're feeling especially creative, try making your child's favorite character.

I've added quinoa flour to this recipe for extra protein, which is great for sustained energy and concentration. Quinoa contains a balanced set of <u>essential amino acids,</u> making it an unusually complete protein source. Whisking all the healthy ingredients together in this recipe gives your child a great deep pressure sensory experience.

Ingredients

1 tablespoon butter or vegan butter substitute
1 cup rice flour
½ cup quinoa flour
½ tablespoon baking soda
½ teaspoon salt
1 egg
⅓ cup honey (less for less sweet pancakes)
1 cup milk or milk substitute (e.g., rice, almond, soy)
1 teaspoon vanilla extract
Syrup (optional)

Yields 10-12 small pancakes.

Tools

Frying pan	Whisk
1 Large bowl	Spatula
1 Medium-sized bowl	Measuring cups
Large spoon	Measuring spoons
Butter knife	Paper towel

Directions

1. **Prepare the cooking area in advance. Clear all clutter. Set out all ingredients and cooking utensils.**

2. **Read through the entire recipe and instructions (on the CD-ROM or print-outs) with your child, pointing to each word as you read.**

Emphasize words that repeat, like cup, crack, mix, etc. Connect the words to the photos as you talk about what you'll be doing.

3. **Wash hands.**

The sensation of the water will calm and ready your child for cooking. Take advantage of this time to do any last minute prep.

4. **Put a tablespoon of butter into a frying pan and turn on low so it can melt while you mix up the batter.**

Keep an eye on the pan to make sure it's not burning. You want to keep a relaxed pace and work with your child in an unhurried way, so you can always take the pan off the burner if the butter is melted and you are still working on mixing up the batter.

5. **Mix all of the dry ingredients in a large bowl.**

Point to the number amount for each ingredient and say it aloud to encourage number recognition. Ask your child if he added "more" or "less" rice flour than quinoa flour?

Allow your child to scoop the dry ingredients (with clean hands) into the measuring devices and level them off with a butter knife before dumping them into a large bowl.

Have your baking soda and salt already poured into small bowls (with lids for storage) so your child can readily scoop them with measuring spoons. Leveling dry ingredients off with a butter knife is great practice for fine motor skills.

6. **Combine and whisk the wet ingredients (egg, milk, honey, and vanilla extract) in a medium-sized bowl.**

Have your child crack the egg at the bottom of a medium-sized bowl. Let him punch it, stick his thumbs into it, etc. There is no wrong way to do this and he will choose the method that provides the type of sensory input he is seeking.

Have your child pick out the broken eggshell pieces and wipe them onto a paper towel. Then direct him to wash his hands. These activities provide excellent fine motor skill practice.

Provide hand-over-hand help with deep pressure to assist your child in pouring the milk and vanilla extract into the measuring utensils.

Have your child squeeze the honey from the bottle into the measuring cup. The harder it is to do, the more coordination it will require and the greater deep pressure it will provide his sensory system. (Note: You can thinly coat the inside of the measuring cup with oil to allow the honey to slip out easily.)

7. Slowly pour the wet ingredients into the bowl with the dry ingredients and whisk to make a smooth batter.

 Encourage your child to make big circles with the whisk, folding all of the dry stuff into the wet batter. You can model the motion of making big circles in pantomime as he uses the whisk. "Round and round, that's the way…big and round!"

 If the batter looks lumpy, play a turn taking game. Your child can hold the bowl while you take a turn with the whisk. Go back and forth a few times, changing roles.

8. Add batter to the pan with a tablespoon to make Mickey's "head," then make "ears" by adding ½ tablespoon of batter to each side of Mickey's head.

This step and the next one are for adults to do, but children can watch you cook the pancakes from a safe distance.

9. When the pancakes start to bubble around the edges, flip them over with a spatula.

 If your child is watching nearby, you can play up the anticipation of watching for the pancakes to bubble. "They're almost bubbling…here they go…I'm going to flip it!" Watching for the pancakes to bubble can become a moment of joint attention, something that can be difficult for children with autism.

10. Transfer pancakes to a plate. Top with butter, syrup, or honey. Yum!

 Take a moment to blow on the hot pancakes with your child. Ask your child if he can see Mickey's ears. Take a bite and comment on how sweet the syrup is. Think of how many words you can highlight just by eating pancakes together!

Baked Apples

Level II (moderately difficult)

Like a lot of kids with autism, George can be a finicky eater, especially at breakfast time. Last year, he went through a month or so where the only fruit he ate was apples. It was during that time that I tried making baked apples for breakfast one day, and they were a big hit. We added roasted almonds to them for some protein. We also make baked apples into a dessert with frozen "Rice Dream" for a real treat!

This recipe requires a lot of fine motor activity, including slicing, pouring, using a melon baller, and adding just a dash of ingredients. Be patient and let your child test out his emerging skills with this delicious recipe.

Ingredients

2 apples
2 tablespoons raisins (or currants or dried figs)
2 tablespoons butter or vegan butter substitute (softened)
2 tablespoons honey
A dash of cinnamon
Water

Tools

Knife	Measuring spoons
Spoon	Small bowl
Melon baller	Cutting board
Measuring cups	Baking dish

Directions

1. **Prepare the cooking area in advance. Clear all clutter. Set out all ingredients and cooking utensils.**

2. **Read through the entire recipe and instructions (on the CD-ROM or print-outs) with your child, pointing to each word as you read.**

    Emphasize words specific to this recipe, like slice, scoop, pour, etc. Connect the words to the photos as you talk about what you'll be doing.

3. Preheat the oven to 375°.

 Let your child set the temperature with your assistance. Say the numbers aloud as you do this.

4. Wash hands.

 The sensation of the water will calm and ready your child for cooking. Take advantage of this time to do any last minute prep.

5. Wash the apples in the sink.

 Have your child turn the cold water on and count to ten out loud together while rinsing the fruit. Then have him turn off the faucet so as not to waste water.

6. Slice off the top quarter of each apple.

 Use hand-over-hand guidance to slice off the tops of the apples with your child. Save them for snacking or to pack in a lunchbox.

7. Use a melon baller to scoop out the seeds and the cores.

  This is a fun, safe tool for your child to use that will also build hand strength. Let him have a go at it and then take out any seeds that he misses.

8. Place the apples, cut side up, into a baking dish.

 You can use a simple step like this one to work on your child's referencing. That is, give your child the opportunity to observe what you are doing, rather than telling your child what to do. Place one apple in the baking dish and then pause and gesture to your child to take the other apple. Try using nonverbal cues to guide him to place the second apple in the baking dish.

9. In a small bowl, mix the raisins, butter, and honey. Add a dash of cinnamon.

 Provide hand-over-hand help with deep pressure to assist your child in scooping, cutting, and squeezing the raisins, butter, and honey. (Note: You can thinly coat the inside of the measuring spoon with oil to allow the honey to slip out easily.)

 If your child likes the smell of cinnamon, take a moment to hold the jar and let him sniff before allowing him to sprinkle some cinnamon into the honey mixture. You may want to use hand over hand if you think your child might shake out too much cinnamon.

You can experiment with using different spices, like cardamom or nutmeg, with or in place of the cinnamon. Compare different spices with your child by holding up one at a time and inviting him to take a whiff. Orange and lemon juices add nice flavor and aroma.

10. Spoon one half of the mixture into each apple.

 Mixing in this small bowl and spooning carefully into the cored apples is great practice for fine motor coordination.

11. Pour 1 inch of water into the baking dish around the apples.

  Use a measuring cup filled with a small amount of water and guide your child to pour into the dish around the apples. You can pull out a ruler to show your child (on the outside of the pan) whether the water is up to an inch or if you need to add more.

12. Place the baking dish into the oven and bake for 30 minutes.

13. Allow 10 minutes to cool and enjoy!

Almond Butter Muffins

Level III (more difficult)

Almond butter gives these breakfast muffins an important serving of protein, essential for concentration and focus throughout your child's morning. Stirring almond butter into the batter gives your child a nice amount of sensory input. Since these muffins don't take long to bake, you could make them together in the morning before school. You can observe whether doing a cooking activity with lots of fine motor work and sensory input before school helps your child's focus for the rest of the morning.

Ingredients

2 cups almond flour
1 teaspoon baking soda
1 teaspoon salt
1 cup almond butter (or other nut butter)
⅓ cup honey
2 eggs
¼ cup oil (any type)

Yields 12 muffins.

Tools

2 Large bowls
1 Medium-sized bowl
2 large spoons
Butter knife
Measuring cups

Measuring spoons
Muffin tin
Muffin liners (paper)
Paper towel

Directions

1. **Prepare the cooking area in advance. Clear all clutter. Set out all ingredients and cooking utensils.**

2. **Read through the entire recipe and instructions (on the CD-ROM or printouts) with your child, pointing to each word as you read.**

     Emphasize words that repeat, like cup, teaspoon, mix, etc. Connect the words to the photos as you talk about what you'll be doing.

3. Wash hands.

 The sensation of the water will calm and ready your child for cooking. Take advantage of this time to do any last minute prep.

4. Preheat the oven to 350°.

 Let your child set the temperature with your assistance. Say the numbers aloud as you do this.

5. Mix all of the dry ingredients in a large bowl.

  Allow your child to scoop the almond flour into the measuring cup and level it off with a butter knife before dumping it into a large bowl. Have your baking soda and salt already poured into small bowls so that your child can readily scoop them with a measuring spoon and level them off. Leveling dry ingredients off with a butter knife is great practice for fine motor skills.

6. In another large bowl, combine almond butter and honey.

  You may need to use hand over hand to help your child reach into the almond butter jar with a spoon and take out the almond butter. Scoop it into the measuring cup and add more as needed. Use a spoon to transfer it from the measuring cup into the mixing bowl.

   Squeezing honey from a "honey bear" is a fun way to pour out the honey and it provides deep pressure to the muscles while building strength in your child's hands (needed for writing). (Note: You can thinly coat the inside of the measuring cup with oil to allow the honey to slip out easily.)

7. Add the eggs and oil to the almond butter and honey mixture and stir.

 Have your child crack the eggs at the bottom of a medium-sized bowl. Let him punch them, stick his thumbs into them, etc. There is no wrong way to do this and he will choose the method that provides the type of sensory input he is seeking.

 Have your child pick out the broken eggshell pieces and wipe them onto a paper towel. Then direct him to wash his hands. These activities provide excellent fine motor skill practice.

 Your child may need hand-over-hand assistance to pour out the oil. You may want to transfer a small amount of oil into a smaller container to give your child practice pouring, as a large bottle of cooking oil may be too heavy for your child to control.

Have your child steady the bowl on the counter with one arm and stir the mixture with the other. This helps build strength and coordination while providing deep pressure to his joints and muscles.

8. Slowly pour the dry ingredients into the wet ingredients and mix.

Pick up the bowl of dry ingredients and very slowly say "Slooowly" and begin to pour with your child. As you cook together, think about times when you can use the word "fast!" like when you're stirring, and when you need to emphasize "slow." Pouring slowly and giving language to what you are doing creates a context for understanding the difference between fast and slow.

9. Line the muffin tin with paper liners.

Count out how many muffin tins you need to fill together and then count out paper liners together. You can use different color papers to create a pattern. Try yellow, then pink, then yellow, then let your child complete the pattern.

10. Using a big spoon or ladle, scoop out the batter and pour it into the paper liners.

Your child can do the scooping. If batter spills on the tin, just wipe it up. Practice filling the tin from left to right, to reinforce the idea of moving from left to right in reading and writing.

11. Bake at 350° for 15 minutes.

Let your child set the kitchen timer with assistance.

Point out to your child that muffins should become brown around the edges, but not burnt.

12. Cool for 10 minutes.

If you're in a rush to get out the door, put one in a napkin and take it along in the car. Why not pack one for your child's teacher and show him what your child can do in the morning before he even gets to school!

Chicken Wraps

Lunch

Better Than PB & J

Grilled "Cheese" Sandwich

Veggie Veggie Burgers

Sweet Potato Latkes

Chicken Wraps

Level I (easy)

Being a mom of a child with special needs means that my daily schedule is almost always full. Sound familiar? I rely on having a few items available in my fridge and pantry that I can put together for quick meals: gluten-free tortillas and rotisserie or pre-baked chicken are some of my saving graces. These wraps come together quickly and easily, and as your child's fine motor skills improve, I'll bet that before long he'll be able to make these almost independently. Just set out as much or as little of the ingredients as you think you'll eat. We often eat Chicken Wraps for lunch and it's rumored that we've eaten them again a few hours later for dinner too!

Ingredients

Lettuce leaves (pre-washed)
Tomatoes
Baked or roasted chicken breasts
Brown rice tortillas
GF ketchup

Tools

Knife
Cutting board
Colander
Toothpicks

Directions

1. Prepare the cooking area in advance. Clear all clutter. Set out all ingredients and cooking utensils.

2. Read through the entire recipe and instructions (on the CD-ROM or print-outs) with your child, pointing to each word as you read.

    Emphasize words that are specific to this recipe, like rip, chop, roll, etc. Connect the words to the photos as you talk about what you'll be doing.

3. Wash hands.

 The sensation of the water will calm and ready your child for cooking. Take advantage of this time to do any last minute prep, like washing the lettuce leaves.

4. Rip the lettuce into bite-sized pieces.

 This is a quick, fun sensory activity that you can do anytime with your child—that way, you can always have lettuce prepped for salad in your fridge.

5. Wash the tomatoes and cut into bite-sized pieces.

 If using a knife is a new skill for your child, use hand-over-hand and take your time cutting the tomatoes.

6. If the pre-cooked chicken breast is not already cut into small pieces, cut it up.

 You could apply hand-over-hand guidance using a knife with your child or even use a pair of kitchen shears for practice cutting with scissors.

7. Squirt some ketchup in the center of a tortilla.

 This can be a great moment of sensory input and very motivating if your child likes ketchup. (Note: Use any sauce your child likes, e.g., barbeque sauce, mustard, mayo, salsa, or no sauce at all.)

8. Top the tortilla with lettuce, tomatoes, and chicken.

 Picking up the small food pieces and placing them on the tortilla is great fine motor practice. You can do some counting here to help your child keep proportions right. "Let's count out four pieces of lettuce…." Place them down the center of the tortilla and then decide if you need more. Count the tomato and chicken pieces, too.

9. Roll the tortilla into a wrap sandwich.

 Demonstrate for your child how to roll the warp tightly, like a jelly roll. You may want to insert a toothpick to secure it. Your child will probably need assistance with making a tight wrap, especially the first few times that he tries.

10. Eat right away!

 Brainstorm about what other ingredients would go together to make a delicious wrap. Make up a list of vegetable, sauce, and meat combinations and write up your own wrap recipes.

Better Than PB & J

Level I (easy)

Sure, you could just make a nut butter and jelly sandwich on the GFCF bread that your child likes, but this quickly heated sandwich is sooo much tastier. And all the scooping and spreading that this recipe requires is great fine motor practice for your child. Use your child's favorite jam or jelly in place of honey if you prefer. We sometimes add sliced bananas to our sandwiches. If you're feeling inspired, you might even go Elvis on this sandwich and add a slice of bacon or two!

Children who prefer crunchy food may not initially be thrilled about the gooeyness of this sandwich. Try cutting it up and offering small bite-sized pieces to start out.

Ingredients

    1 tablespoon (approximately) nut butter (e.g., almond, cashew, peanut, or soy)
    2 slices GFCF bread
    1 tablespoon (approximately) honey
    1 teaspoon butter or vegan butter substitute

Tools

    2 Butter knives
    Spatula
    Skillet
    Kitchen timer

Directions

1. **Prepare the cooking area in advance. Clear all clutter. Set out all ingredients and cooking utensils.**

2. **Read through the entire recipe and instructions (on the CD-ROM or print-outs) with your child, pointing to each word as you read.**

    Emphasize words that repeat, like scoop and spread. Connect the words to the photos as you talk about what you'll be doing.

3. **Wash hands.**

    The sensation of the water will calm and ready your child for preparing a meal. Take advantage of this time to do any last minute prep.

4. Spread nut butter on one piece of bread and spread or squeeze honey onto the other piece of bread. Make a sandwich.

> Set out two slices of your child's favorite GFCF bread on the kitchen counter or a plate.

 Let your child unscrew the jar, dip a knife in, and scoop out some nut butter. You may need to use hand-over-hand to help.

 Spreading with a knife is a wonderful way for your child to practice fine motor control. If he is enjoying spreading and is doing well with it, have your child make a second sandwich for you!

 If your honey came in a "honey bear," squeezing it out provides deep pressure to your child's muscles while building strength in his hands (needed for writing).

 If your child prefers jelly or jam to honey, make a sandwich with that variation. This simple recipe is a great way to play with variations—make a list of all of the different nut butter and honey/jam/jelly variations that you can try.

5. Heat butter (or substitute) in your skillet over medium heat and place the sandwich into the skillet.

> Your child can watch from a safe distance. Cook for approximately 4 minutes on each side or until golden brown.

 Help your child to set a kitchen timer for three minutes and when the timer goes off, check and see if the bread is golden brown. If it is, flip the sandwich with a spatula. If not, set the timer for another minute.

6. Let the sandwich cool down on a plate for another 3-4 minutes.

> Burning your tongue never makes for a happy lunch.

Grilled "Cheese" Sandwich

Level 1 (easy)

It's really important to me that my son still gets to eat classic childhood comfort foods, like grilled cheese, even though his diet excludes gluten. We used to use vegan cheese but now George is tolerating dairy products so we use real cheddar. Either way, a grilled cheese sandwich makes a cozy meal in the middle of a busy day.

This recipe offers a concrete opportunity to focus on the number two: two pieces of bread, two slices of cheese, and two tablespoons of butter.

Ingredients

2 slices GFCF bread
2 slices vegan cheese (or cheddar if your child can tolerate it)
2 tablespoons butter or vegan butter substitute

Tools

Plate
Spatula
Skillet
Kitchen timer

Directions

1. **Prepare the cooking area in advance. Clear all clutter. Set out all ingredients and cooking utensils.**

2. **Read through the entire recipe and instructions (on the CD-ROM or print-outs) with your child, pointing to each word as you read.**
     Emphasize words and phrases that are specific to this recipe, like "on top," and the number 2. Connect the words to the photos as you talk about what you'll be doing.

3. **Wash hands.**
     The sensation of the water will calm and ready your child for cooking. Take advantage of this time to do any last minute prep.

4. **Put two slices of cheese on a piece of bread and cover to make a sandwich.**
     Offer your child several pieces of bread and ask him to select just two. Then do the same with slices of cheese.

5. **Heat butter (or substitute) in your skillet and place the sandwich into the skillet.**

 Help your child slice off two tablespoons of butter or measure out two tablespoons of a vegan substitute.

6. **Cook the sandwich for approximately 4 minutes on each side or until golden brown.**

 Help your child to set a timer for three minutes and when the timer goes off, check and see if the bread is golden brown. If it is, flip the sandwich with a spatula and if not, set the time for another minute.

7. **Let the sandwich cool down on a plate for another 3-4 minutes.**

  Point out how the cheese looks different after it's been cooked...it's melted. Discuss other things that change form after they've been heated.

Veggie Veggie Burgers

Level II (moderately difficult)

Making Veggie Veggie Burgers is a perfect midday sensory break! Your child gets to mash, grate, peel, and pound to his or her heart's content. Veggie Veggie Burgers also make a quick, easy, inexpensive and delicious lunch for the whole family. As with all of the recipes in *The Kitchen Classroom,* feel free to substitute vegetables that your child prefers. This recipe calls for mild seasoning, but if the adults in your home like a spicier burger, top with some hot sauce. We serve these veggie burgers on GFCF rolls or buns, although my kids also like eating them right out of the skillet and onto their plates.

Ingredients

1 15-ounce can black beans
1 bell pepper (any color)
2 scallions
1 carrot
1 egg
1 cup GFCF crackers (crushed)
Salt and pepper to taste
1 tablespoon olive oil (approximately)
GFCF rolls or buns

Yields 8 veggie burgers.

Tools

Large spoon	Cutting board
Knife	1 Big bowl
Can opener	1 Medium-sized bowl
Grater	Plate
Peeler	Paper towel
Spatula	Plastic zip top sandwich bag
Potato masher	Frying pan
Colander	

Directions

1. **Prepare the cooking area in advance. Clear all clutter. Set out all ingredients and cooking utensils.**

2. **Read through the entire recipe and instructions (on the CD-ROM or print-outs) with your child, pointing to each word as you read.**

 Emphasize words that are specific to this recipe, like grate, peel, pound, etc. Connect the words to the photos as you talk about what you'll be doing.

3. **Wash hands.**

 The sensation of the water will calm and ready your child for cooking. Take advantage of this time to do any last minute prep.

4. **Open the can of beans, rinse them in a colander under cold water, and drain them.**

 Remove the lid yourself, as the edges will be sharp, and allow your child to dump the beans into a colander in the sink and turn on the cold water. Then have your child dump the rinsed beans into a bowl.

5. **Mash rinsed and drained beans in a bowl.**

 Let your child dump the beans into a large bowl and use hand-over-hand to help him mash them with a potato masher. This works the large muscles of the trunk and provides soothing deep pressure.

6. **Wash and chop the bell pepper and scallions, then add to the beans.**

 The sensation of the water will focus your child on the activity at hand.

 If using a knife is a new skill for your child, use hand-over-hand and take your time cutting the vegetables. You can use turn-taking to model chopping. When it's your child's turn, give him encouragement and label what he's doing, "You are chopping! Great chopping!" When it's your turn, you can cut the vegetables into smaller pieces than your child may be able to.

7. **Peel and grate the carrot, then add to the bean mixture.**

 If a peeler and grater are new tools for your child, keep in mind that the first time with a new tool may feel awkward for your child. Be patient and help your child with hand-over-hand as needed. Peeling and grating the carrot may be too much work the first time that you try this recipe, so this step could also be an opportunity to practice turn-taking by passing the carrot back and forth until it is prepared.

8. **Crack the egg into a medium-sized bowl, then add it to the bean-veggie mixture.**

> Have your child crack the egg at the bottom of a medium-sized bowl. Let him punch it, stick his thumbs into it, etc. There is no wrong way to do this and he will choose the method that provides the type of sensory input he is seeking.

> Have your child pick out the broken eggshell pieces and wipe them onto a paper towel. Then direct him to wash his hands. These activities provide excellent fine motor skill practice.

9. **Put crackers into a sealed plastic bag and crush them. Then add the crushed crackers to the bean-veggie mixture and stir.**

> This step can be so much fun for you and your child! Have him smash the bag between his hands, or make a fist and pound the crackers against your kitchen counter. Of course, you could roll over the bag with a rolling pin, but in our house, we prefer the more rugged approach!

> After dumping the crushed crackers into the mixture, have your child steady the bowl on the counter with one arm and stir the mixture with the other. This helps build strength and coordination while providing deep pressure to his joints and muscles.

10. **Take small amounts of the mixture and press firmly in your hands to make patties.**

> For children who are sensory avoidant, they may be hesitant to press this mixture in their hands. First, invite them to watch you make a patty. Then see if they will touch a small amount. Give lots of encouragement. Remember, it might take several times making this recipe before a sensory avoidant child will get his hands into the mix.

> Place the patties onto a plate as you make them. Add salt and pepper to taste.

11. **Pour a small amount of olive oil to coat the bottom of the frying pan and heat over high.**

> Your child can watch from a safe distance as you cook the veggie burgers. Lightly fry each side (3-4 minutes).

> Explain that you are waiting for the heat to cook each side and turn the patties lightly brown.

Sweet Potato Latkes

Level III (more difficult)

Latkes, or potato pancakes, are a traditional Jewish food served at Chanukah, the festival of lights. Latkes are cooked in oil to commemorate the oil that was used to rededicate the ancient Temple in Jerusalem. My husband, Fred, and I host an annual Chanukah party for his side of the family. When George started the GFCF diet I was happy to discover that rice flour makes wonderfully light latkes. For this recipe, have your child grate the potatoes—this is a great upper body workout! Although we love latkes at Chanukah, we also make these latkes from time to time for a weekend lunch.

Ingredients

    3-4 large sweet potatoes
    3-4 medium red potatoes
    2 eggs
    1 onion (pre-grated)
    1 teaspoon salt
    1 teaspoon cinnamon
    ½ teaspoon pepper
    ⅓ cup rice flour
    ¾ cup olive oil (approximately)

Yields 12-15 small latkes.

Tools

Grater	1 Large bowl
Clean unused sponge or vegetable scrubber	1 Medium-sized bowl
Spatula	Colander
Large spoon	Paper towel
Butter knife	Large plate or cookie sheet
Measuring cups	Frying pan
Measuring spoons	

Directions

1. **Prepare the cooking area in advance. Clear all clutter. Set out all ingredients and cooking utensils.**

2. **Read through the entire recipe and instructions (on the CD-ROM or print-outs) with your child, pointing to each word as you read.**

 Emphasize words that are specific to this recipe, like squeeze, shred, mix, etc. Connect the words to the photos as you talk about what you'll be doing.

3. **Wash hands.**

 The sensation of the water will calm and ready your child for cooking. Take advantage of this time to do any last minute prep, like grating the onion.

4. **Wash and scrub potatoes.**

 Arm your child with a vegetable scrubber or clean sponge and let him go to town cleaning the potatoes under cold water. My grandmother always kept the skin on potatoes, insisting that the skin had the most nutrients of the potato, so I tend to follow her lead. If you're using organic potatoes, the peel is especially safe to eat. If not, you may want to peel your potatoes before starting the recipe with your child.

 As you wash the potatoes, count them with your child. "One potato, two potatoes, three potatoes…."

5. **Grate the potatoes with a hand grater.**

 This takes a lot of hand strength and plenty of patience! Work hand-over-hand with your child. If he can grate 1-2 potatoes with you, that is excellent! When he gets tired, give your child a break while you finish the potatoes on your own. I like to make this recipe when everyone in the family is home, so two of us adults can grate the potatoes quickly when my kids burn out.

6. **Pour the potatoes into a colander and drain off excess liquid.**

 Show your child how to press down hard on the shredded potato to squeeze out the liquid. This helps build up his strength and coordination while providing deep pressure to his joints and muscles.

This step is essential to the success of your latkes! Once drained, pour the potatoes back into a large bowl.

7. **Crack the eggs and add them to the potato mixture.**

 Have your child crack the eggs at the bottom of a medium-sized bowl. Let him punch them, stick his thumbs into them, etc. There is no wrong way to do this and he will choose the method that provides the type of sensory input he is seeking.

Have your child pick out the broken eggshell pieces and wipe them onto a paper towel. Then direct him to wash his hands. These activities provide excellent fine motor skill practice.

8. Add the onions, salt, pepper, cinnamon, and flour to the potatoes and mix.

I grate the onion in advance because I have found that my children are too sensitive and tear up when grating an onion. Have your child dump the grated onion into the potato mixture.

 Provide hand-over-hand help with deep pressure to assist your child in scooping the salt, pepper, and cinnamon into the measuring spoons and leveling them off with a butter knife. Have these ingredients already poured into small bowls so that your child can readily scoop them.

 Allow your child to scoop the flour into the measuring device and level it off before dumping it into the bowl with the other ingredients.

 Stir the mixture with a large spoon until everything is incorporated. When we're making latkes, I like to sing Chanukah songs with my children. I find that as I sing slowly it helps George coordinate his actions and stir slowly. (If you're not Jewish, you can pick any song or make up a song about stirring!)

9. Heat the olive oil in a frying pan over high heat. The oil should be a centimeter or so deep.

Your child can watch the action from a safe distance.

10. Drop a spoonful of potato mixture into the oil and flatten with a spatula to make loose patties.

Fry until the bottom begins to brown and then flip to the other side with a spatula. When the latke is golden brown on both sides, transfer to a plate or cookie sheet covered with paper towel to absorb the excess oil.

 When the latkes are ready, count them with your child. Recall how many potatoes you counted earlier. Marvel at how many latkes can come out of a few potatoes!

 Sesame Salmon

Pizza Pie

Dinner

 Chicken Sauté

 Fried Rice & Veggies

 Mama's Meatballs

 Nut Butter Noodles

 Rice Noodle Lasagna

Sesame Salmon

Level I (easy)

My husband and I love eating seafood—especially in the summer when we put fresh tilapia or flounder on the grill. The only fish that our kids will eat at the moment, though, is salmon. Hey—it's a start. We make wild Alaskan salmon at least once a week and appreciate not only its delicious flavor but the benefits of its omega-3 fatty acids. Many doctors recommend supplementing the diets of children with autism and ADHD with omega-3 fatty acids because studies show that it improves cognition when tested in animals.

Ingredients

    3 (6-ounce) wild Alaskan salmon fillets
    3 teaspoons olive oil
    2 lemons
    2 tablespoons honey
    2 teaspoons sea salt
    Sesame seeds (approximately 1 teaspoon per filet)

Tools

Butter Knife	Juicer
Knife	Small bowl
Spoon	Cutting board
Measuring spoons	Roasting pan	Kitchen timer

Directions

1. **Prepare the cooking area in advance. Clear all clutter. Set out all ingredients and cooking utensils.**

2. **Read through the entire recipe and instructions (on the CD-ROM or print-outs) with your child, pointing to each word as you read.**

    Emphasize words that are specific to this recipe, like squeeze, pour, sprinkle, etc. Connect the words to the photos as you talk about what you'll be doing.

3. **Wash hands.**

    The sensation of the water will calm and ready your child for cooking. Take advantage of this time to do any last minute prep.

4. Preheat oven to 350°.

Let your child set the temperature with your assistance. Say the numbers aloud as you do this.

5. Place the salmon in a roasting pan.

Sensory avoidant children may not want to experience the texture of salmon with bare hands at first. That's okay—just have them watch. Children who are extra sensitive to smell may be put off by a "fishy" smell. In fact, fish that is fresh should not have a fishy smell. I often buy frozen wild alaskan salmon that has a neutral smell.

Direct your child to wash his hands after touching raw fish.

6. Cover each fillet of salmon with 1 teaspoon of olive oil.

Use hand-over-hand to measure out and pour the olive oil over the fish.

7. Combine the juice of the lemons, with the honey and salt, and stir.

(Note: Sea salt has minerals that provide extra health benefits, but using regular table salt for this recipe is fine.)

Use hand-over-hand to help your child cut the lemons in half and then juice them into a small bowl. Make sure that no seeds get in. Squeezing a juicer is great sensory and gross motor work, as is squeezing honey from a "honey bear." (Note: You can thinly coat the inside of the measuring spoon with oil to allow the honey to slip out easily.)

Have your salt already poured into a small bowl (with lid for storage) so your child can readily scoop it with a measuring spoon. Leveling dry ingredients off with a butter knife is great practice for fine motor skills, as is stirring wet ingredients carefully with a spoon.

8. Pour the lemon juice-honey mixture over salmon.

Use hand-over-hand guidance with your child to pour the lemon juice-honey mixture over each of the fillets.

Point out that there are three pieces of fish, so you want to use ⅓ of the mixture on each piece of fish.

9. Sprinkle sesame seeds on top of the salmon to form a crust.

Your child can use his hands to sprinkle. The seeds don't need to be perfectly even or cover all of the fillets.

10. Bake at 350° for 30 minutes.

 Let your child set the kitchen timer with assistance.

11. Take the fish out of the oven and let sit for 10 minutes before serving.

This dish is delicious served over rice, quinoa, or polenta.

Chicken Sauté

Level I (easy)

Before we started George on a GFCF diet, the only protein that I could get him to eat was McDonald's chicken nuggets. (I use the term "protein" very loosely here.) This concerned me, because as a mother and a professional cooking instructor, I know how essential protein is for a growing child, especially to keep the immune system healthy and all of the organs strong. Amazingly, when we took gluten out of George's diet, he became open to tasting and then regularly eating protein. Chicken is his favorite source and this quick, simple sauté is his favorite way to eat it.

Ingredients

Olive oil (1 tablespoon per chicken breast)
Chicken breast (1 per person)
Sea salt (1 teaspoon per chicken breast)
Dried basil (1 teaspoon per chicken breast) (optional)

Tools

Butter Knife
Kitchen shears
Tongs
Measuring spoons
Medium-sized bowl
Frying pan

Directions

1. **Prepare the cooking area in advance. Clear all clutter. Set out all ingredients and cooking utensils.**

2. **Read through the entire recipe and instructions (on the CD-ROM or print-outs) with your child, pointing to each word as you read.**

    Emphasize words that are specific to this recipe, like cut, wash, sprinkle, etc. Connect the words to the photos as you talk about what you'll be doing.

3. **Wash hands.**

    The sensation of the water will calm and ready your child for cooking. Take advantage of this time to do any last minute prep.

4. Measure and pour the olive oil into the frying pan and turn on high heat.

Use hand-over-hand guidance with your child to measure out and pour the olive oil into the cold pan. Your child can watch as you put the skillet on the stove and turn the stove on high.

5. Use kitchen shears to cut the chicken breast into bite-sized pieces. Put the chicken pieces into a bowl.

This is a great opportunity for teamwork! My role is to hold the chicken breast while George uses the shears to snip it into small pieces. It's lots of fun to work together and we've gotten better over time!

Direct your child to wash his hands after touching raw meat.

6. Sprinkle the chicken pieces with sea salt.

(Note: Sea salt has minerals that provide extra health benefits, but using regular table salt for this recipe is fine.)

Have your salt already poured into a small bowl (with lid for storage) so your child can readily scoop it with a measuring spoon. Leveling dry ingredients off with a butter knife is great practice for fine motor skills.

Add any spices that your family likes at this point.

7. Carefully place the chicken pieces into the hot skillet. Use tongs to turn them over. Cook on each side for 3-5 minutes until lightly browned.

You can cut a piece in the middle to make sure that it is cooked through. If it is still a little pick, sauté for another 3-4 minutes and check again.

Meanwhile, your child can watch from a safe distance while you sauté. Sometimes my kids sit down and start eating vegetables (think ABC Salad) while I quickly sauté, then serve.

8. Let sit for 3-4 minutes to cool slightly.

Serving something like a hot chicken breast can be a good time to practice how to blooooow on food. No burnt tongues, please!

Fried Rice & Veggies

Level II (moderately difficult)

I hate wasting food. Paying for my son's therapies on top of our monthly bills leaves me a limited budget to spend on groceries, so I try to make use of everything that I buy. This simple recipe for fried rice is a great way to use up leftover rice. (And all the chopping gives your child a great fine motor work-out!) It's full of aromatic smells and cooks up quickly. Toss in leftover chicken or turkey and use up whatever vegetables are starting to get mushy in your produce drawer.

Ingredients

> 2 tablespoons olive or sesame oil
> 4 scallions
> 2 bell peppers (red, green, or yellow)
> 2-3 stalks of celery
> 2 cloves garlic
> 3 cups cooked brown rice
> 3 tablespoons GF tamari sauce
>
> *Yields 3-4 servings.*

Tools

> Knife
> Wooden spoon
> Measuring spoons
> Garlic press
> Cutting board
> Skillet or wok

Directions

1. **Prepare the cooking area in advance. Clear all clutter. Set out all ingredients and cooking utensils.**

2. **Read through the entire recipe and instructions (on the CD-ROM or print-outs) with your child, pointing to each word as you read.**

 Emphasize words that repeat, like tablespoon, chop, peel, etc. Connect the words to the photos as you talk about what you'll be doing.

3. Wash hands.

 The sensation of the water will calm and ready your child for cooking. Take advantage of this time to do any last minute prep.

4. Measure and pour oil into the skillet. (Let the skillet sit cold on your counter while you work on the vegetables.)

 Provide hand-over-hand guidance to measure out and pour the olive oil into the pan.

5. Wash and chop the scallions, bell peppers, and celery. Then add the veggies to the cold skillet.

 The sensation of the water will focus your child on the activity at hand.

 If using a knife is a new skill for your child, use hand-over-hand and take your time cutting the vegetables. You can use turn-taking to model chopping. When it's your child's turn, give him encouragement and label what he's doing, "You are chopping! Great chopping!" When it's your turn, you can cut the vegetables into smaller pieces than your child may be able to. Then dump the chopped veggies into the skillet.

 Your child can break the celery stalks into pieces with his hands—this is a great sensory workout! After they're broken into big chunks, you can chop them into smaller pieces, and add them to the skillet.

6. Take the skins off of the garlic cloves, place in a garlic press, and squeeze straight into the cold skillet.

  Taking the peel off of the garlic cloves is great practice for fine motor skills, but can be a frustrating job, so stand by to give help. Squeezing a garlic press is great fun and great sensory and gross motor work!

7. Put the skillet on the stove over high heat and cook the vegetables while stirring for 5 minutes, or until they soften.

If your child is interested in watching, he can stand on a chair at a safe distance. I like to keep coloring books and crayons in the kitchen so that my kids can opt out when their part of the cooking is done. They can stay busy but be within my gaze while I do the stir-fry part.

8. Add the already-cooked brown rice and let it heat through while stirring occasionally for another 5 minutes.

9. Stir in the tamari sauce and serve onto plates right from the pan.

Leftovers never tasted so good!

Mama's Meatballs

Level II (moderately difficult)

Mama's Meatballs are yummy to eat with spaghetti or just right from the baking sheet onto a plate. This is a real hands-on recipe—great for getting sensory input. If your kids enjoy making meatballs as much as mine do, you can make an extra batch and put a portion in the freezer for another day.

In our house, we have a spaghetti and meatballs night every month that my kids look forward to. Mark it on your calendar and make a big deal of dinner. Try serving special drinks and dessert. With a little attention to detail, you can create a little restaurant experience right in your own home!

Ingredients

1 teaspoon olive oil (approximately)
1 pound ground beef or ground turkey
1 cup GFCF crackers (crushed)
2 eggs
1 teaspoon salt
1 teaspoon pepper
1 teaspoon garlic powder

Yields 2 dozen meatballs.

Tools

Butter knife	1 Large bowl
Large spoon	1 Medium-sized bowl
Measuring spoons	Baking sheet
Measuring cups	Paper towel
Plastic zip top sandwich bag	Kitchen timer

Directions

1. **Prepare the cooking area in advance. Clear all clutter. Set out all ingredients and cooking utensils.**

2. **Read through the entire recipe and instructions (on the CD-ROM or printouts) with your child, pointing to each word as you read.**

   Emphasize words that repeat, like cup, teaspoon, mix, etc. Connect the words to the photos as you talk about what you'll be doing.

3. Wash hands.

The sensation of the water will calm and ready your child for cooking. Take advantage of this time to do any last minute prep.

4. Preheat oven to 350°.

Let your child set the temperature with your assistance. Say the numbers aloud as you do this.

5. Lightly grease a baking sheet with olive oil.

I pour some olive oil onto a paper towel and show my son how to rub the paper towel back and forth across the pan.

6. Open the package of ground meat and pour into a large bowl.

A pound of ground beef or turkey may be heavy for your child to hold and dump. Show him how to use two hands and be ready to assist if needed.

Direct him to wash his hands if they get raw meat on them.

7. Smash some crackers in a sealed plastic bag. Then measure out 1 cup and dump them into the bowl with the ground meat.

This step can be SO much fun for your child! Give him the freedom to smash the bag between his hands, or make a fist and pound the crackers against the kitchen counter. Of course, he could roll over the bag with a rolling pin, but in our house, we prefer the more rugged approach!

Allow your child to scoop the crushed crackers into the measuring cup and level it off with his hands before dumping them into the bowl with the meat.

8. Crack the eggs into a medium-sized bowl then add them into the ground meat mixture.

Have your child crack the eggs at the bottom of a medium-sized bowl. Let him punch them, stick his thumbs into them, etc. There is no wrong way to do this and he will choose the method that provides the type of sensory input he is seeking.

Have your child pick out the broken eggshell pieces and wipe them onto a paper towel. Then direct him to wash his hands. These activities provide excellent fine motor skill practice.

9. **Add the salt, pepper, and garlic powder to the meat mixture and stir to combine.**

 Have your salt, pepper, and garlic powder already poured into small bowls (with lids for storage) so your child can readily scoop them with measuring spoons. Leveling dry ingredients off with a butter knife is great practice for fine motor skills.

 Help your child steady the bowl on the counter with one hand and stir with the other. This helps build strength and coordination while providing deep pressure to his joints and muscles.

10. **Take a small amount of the meat mixture and roll it into a ball between your hands. Repeat. Evenly space the meatballs on the baking sheet.**

 If your child knows how to roll balls from playing with play dough, show him how to take a little bit of meat in his hands and roll it the same way. Try not to be a perfectionist about the size of the meatballs—some will be bigger and some smaller. When he finishes rolling, ask him to wash his hands.

11. **Bake at 350° for 25-30 minutes.**

 Let your child set the kitchen timer with assistance.

12. **Your meatballs are ready to eat!**

These meatballs are delicious with GFCF pasta and marinara, over brown rice with soy sauce, or just as is!

Nut Butter Noodles

Level II (moderately difficult)

Nut Butter Noodles make a quick, delicious dinner—and an alternative to serving gluten-free pasta with marinara sauce. If you have time, you can make the sauce in the morning, and cut the veggies and boil the pasta just before dinner. All the slicing and dicing in this recipe helps your child develop his fine motor skills. Because my children wake early (between five and six o'clock in the morning), we often prep dinner in the morning, which gives us the opportunity to experience cooking and each others' company before we go off in our different directions.

Ingredients

1 16-ounce package GFCF noodles
1 cucumber
2 carrots
2 scallions
¼ cup nut butter (e.g., almond, cashew, peanut, or soy)
2 tablespoons honey
3 tablespoons brown rice vinegar
3 tablespoons GF tamari sauce
Chili powder or hot sauce for added zing (optional)

Yields 5-6 servings.

Tools

Knife	2 Medium-sized bowls
Large spoon	1 Large bowl
Peeler	Cutting board
Measuring cups	Large cooking pot
Measuring spoons	Colander

Directions

1. **Prepare the cooking area in advance. Clear all clutter. Set out all ingredients and cooking utensils.**

2. **Read through the entire recipe and instructions (on the CD-ROM or print-outs) with your child, pointing to each word as you read.**

 Emphasize words that repeat, like wash, cut, tablespoon, etc. Connect the words to the photos as you talk about what you'll be doing.

3. **Wash hands.**

 The sensation of the water will calm and ready your child for cooking. Take advantage of this time to do any last minute prep.

4. **Fill a large pot ¾ of the way full with water and put on the stove to boil over high heat.**

 Point to imaginary ¼, ½, ¾, and full lines on your cooking pot and discuss fractions. Ask your child to fill the pot to the ¾ line without assistance and see how he does. Then discuss whether you need "more" or "less" water.

 Assist your child in carrying the heavy pot to the stove. This "heavy work" feels great to kids who have sensory processing issues.

5. **Wash, peel, then slice the cucumber, carrots, and scallions.**

  Use hand-over-hand assistance to cut the cucumber length-wise so that the two halves will lay flat on your cutting board. Then cut the cucumber across to make half-moon shaped pieces. (I keep the skin on when using organic cucumbers but suggest peeling conventionally grown cucumbers.) Help your child to peel the carrots and then cut into thin coins. Peeling carrots is a great sensory workout! Help your child cut the green onion into small pieces; discard any loose skin. Use some of the green and some of the white part of the onions.

Place all of the sliced vegetables into a bowl and set aside.

6. **In another bowl, combine the nut butter, honey, vinegar, and tamari sauce.**

  Scooping out the nut butter will take some hand strength, as will squeezing honey from a "honey bear." (Note: You can thinly coat the inside of the measuring spoon with oil to allow the honey to slip out easily.) As you add each ingredient, this will become a thick mixture for your child to stir.

7. When the water comes to a boil, add the pasta and cook according to package directions.

 This is a grown-up job, but it can be interesting for your child to watch you add pasta to the boiling water from a safe distance. Explain that water bubbles when it is boiling. (It's also good to mention that boiling water is very hot and not safe to touch.)

 When your pasta is cooked, drain it in a colander, then have your child help you dump it into a large bowl.

8. Add sauce and vegetables to the pasta and stir.

 Ask your child to dump in the remaining ingredients. Then help him steady the bowl on the counter with one hand and stir with the other. This helps build strength and coordination while providing deep pressure to his joints and muscles.

Your Nut Butter Noodles are ready to eat!

Rice Noodle Lasagna

Level III (more difficult)

If you're looking for a traditional lasagna recipe, this isn't it. But what I have put together is a tasty way to use gluten-free lasagna noodles while you teach your child about fractions and making patterns: "Sauce, noodles, mushrooms, cheese… sauce, noodles, mushrooms, cheese…." It has been exciting for me to watch as George has learned to follow the pattern and assemble the lasagna with almost total independence. Now that he is eating dairy, we do add in a layer of ricotta cheese on top of the noodles. If your child has an aversion to mushrooms, try eggplant or even roasted bell peppers instead.

Ingredients

    1 large package of mushrooms, approximately 16 ounces (e.g., button, porcini)
    1 26-ounce jar GFCF marinara sauce
    GFCF lasagna noodles (my favorite is Tinkayada)
    1 16-ounce package shredded vegan cheese (or mozzarella if your child eats dairy)

Tools

Knife	Colander
Large spoon	Lasagna pan (12" x 18" x 3")
Spatula	Aluminum foil
Cutting board	Kitchen timer

Directions

1. **Prepare the cooking area in advance. Clear all clutter. Set out all ingredients and cooking utensils.**

2. **Read through the entire recipe and instructions (on the CD-ROM or print-outs) with your child, pointing to each word as you read.**

   Emphasize words that repeat, like one quarter, one third, sprinkle, etc. Explain to your child that you'll be creating a pattern with the ingredients. Connect the words to the photos as you talk about what you'll be doing.

3. **Wash hands.**

   The sensation of the water will calm and ready your child for cooking. Take advantage of this time to do any last minute prep.

4. Preheat the oven to 375°.

Let your child set the temperature with your assistance. Say the numbers aloud as you do this.

5. Wash mushrooms in a colander and then cut into bite-sized pieces.

Have your child rinse the mushrooms under cold water, inspecting them for any excess dirt.

Using hand-over-hand assistance with your child, chop the mushrooms with a small knife.

6. In a lasagna pan, pour out ¼ of the jar of marina sauce to cover the bottom of the pan.

Let your child unscrew the marinara jar. You may need to use hand-over-hand to help.

This is a great time to introduce fractions. Use a piece of masking tape to mark the outside of the jar of sauce into quarters. Use hand-over-hand guidance to hold the jar and slowly pour out the sauce to the first quarter mark.

7. Place a single layer of lasagna noodles to cover the sauce.
(Note: in this recipe, you do not need to pre-boil the noodles.)

Explain to your child that you'll be creating a pattern with the ingredients: sauce, noodles, mushrooms, cheese, etc. Lay out the items that you need in order on your counter so you can point to them while saying, "Sauce…noodles…mushrooms…cheese. First we put in the sauce, next we'll put in the…." Gesture to the item that you need and allow your child to select it. If he picks up the wrong item, help him put it down and redirect him, pointing out the pattern again. Begin a rhythmic chant: "Here go the noodles, the noodles, the noodles…" as your child places the noodles in the pan.

8. Sprinkle ⅓ of the cut mushrooms over the lasagna noodles.

Divide the mushrooms into thirds on the cutting board or countertop with your child's help. Use this visual to explain that three thirds equals one whole.

Keep chanting, "Next come the mushrooms, mushrooms, mushrooms…" as you show your child how to sprinkle the mushrooms on top of the noodles.

9. Sprinkle ⅓ of the shredded cheese over the mushrooms.

 Pour the cheese out onto a clean cutting board or countertop and divide it into thirds. Use this visual to demonstrate again that three thirds equals one whole.

 Chant: "Last comes the cheese, the cheese, the cheese…" as you demonstrate sprinkling a layer of shredded cheese.

10. Repeat the layering process with your child two more times, ending with the last quarter of sauce.

11. Cover the lasagna pan with foil.

 Foil is a fun thing to roll out together slowly and carefully. Eyeball the pan and then start to roll the foil. Stop when you have about half of the pan covered and ask your child if you need more foil. You can slowly roll more and pause again, giving your child room to say, sign, or gesture that you need more.

 When you have the right size piece, help your child tear it off and fold the foil over the edges of the pan. Think of language you can use to describe that action…crinkle the foil works well.

12. Place lasagna in the oven to bake for 1 hour.

 Have your child set the kitchen timer with assistance.

13. Remove lasagna from the oven and take off foil. Let lasagna sit for 15 minutes before serving.

 Enjoy the smell of the lasagna permeating your kitchen!

Pizza Pie

Level III (more difficult)

For parents of kids on the GFCF diet, picking up the phone and ordering a pizza for a last minute meal isn't really an option. Luckily, making pizza is a fun and delicious activity. My family loves the smell of pizza baking in the oven!

An important skill that you can emphasize when making this recipe is learning about time. Making pizza is a perfect opportunity to draw your child's attention to the numbers on your kitchen clock. First you'll have to wait for the yeast to dissolve, then for the dough to rise, and again for the crust to bake. Hopefully, you and your children will find this recipe is worth waiting for!

Ingredients

1¼ cup warm water
2 tablespoons rapid dissolve yeast
   (Note: some GFCF pizza crust mixes come with pre-measured yeast)
2 eggs
3 tablespoons olive oil
3 cups GFCF pizza crust mix (I like 'Bob's Red Mill' best)
1 tablespoon butter or butter substitute for greasing pan
1 26-ounce jar GFCF marinara sauce
1 cup shredded cheese or vegan cheese substitute
Toppings, e.g., pre-cut veggies, pepperoni, etc. (optional)

Tools

Butter knife	1 Medium-sized bowl
1 Fork	Paper towel
2 Large spoons	Plastic wrap
Measuring cups	Kitchen timer
Measuring spoons	Pizza pan (16") or baking sheet
1 Large bowl	

Directions

1. **Prepare the cooking area in advance. Clear all clutter. Set out all ingredients and cooking utensils.**

2. **Read through the entire recipe and instructions (on the CD-ROM or print-outs) with your child, pointing to each word as you read.**

 Emphasize words that repeat, like cup, teaspoon, mix, etc. Connect the words to the photos as you talk about what you'll be doing.

3. **Wash hands.**

 The sensation of the water will calm and ready your child for cooking. Take advantage of this time to do any last minute prep, like washing and pre-cutting optional veggie toppings.

4. **Preheat oven to 425°.**

 Let your child set the temperature with your assistance. Say the numbers aloud as you do this.

5. **In a large bowl, combine warm water and yeast. Let stand for a few minutes.**

  Your child can measure out warm water from the tap and pour it into a bowl. Then direct him to open the yeast packet and mix it into the water with a fork. Explain that the warm water is waking the inactive yeast up. Set a timer for three minutes and wait for the yeast to bubble before you start the next step. Count the bubbles while you wait!

6. **Add eggs and oil to the yeast mixture and stir.**

 Have your child crack the eggs at the bottom of a medium-sized bowl. Let him punch them, stick his thumbs into them, etc. There is no wrong way to do this and he will choose the method that provides the type of sensory input he is seeking.

 Have your child pick out the broken eggshell pieces and wipe them onto a paper towel. Then direct him to wash his hands. These activities provide excellent fine motor skill practice.

 You can pre-pour the oil into a smaller pitcher or cup so that it is easier for your child to pour into a measuring spoon.

7. **Add pizza crust mix to the wet ingredients and work into a dough.**

  Allow your child to scoop the dry mix into the measuring cup and level it off with a butter knife before dumping it into the large bowl. Leveling dry ingredients off with a butter knife is great practice for fine motor skills. Have your child add one cup of the dry mix at a time and use a large spoon to mix it in.

Once all of the mix is in the bowl, take turns working the dough with your hands until it becomes smooth. This "messy" activity is a great one for a child with tactile defensiveness because it helps build up tolerance for textures while incorporating some deep pressure therapy.

8. Cover bowl with plastic wrap and leave to rise in a warm spot for 20 minutes.

 Making pizza is an excellent time to draw your child's attention to the numbers on a clock or a kitchen timer, since you have to wait and keep track of time often in the process of making the pizza.

9. Place dough on a greased pizza pan or baking sheet and spread out until it is about ¼-½" thick.

 Give your child a pat of butter (or shortening of your choice) and let him go to town rubbing it onto the pizza pan or baking sheet.

 Flattening and stretching out the pizza dough will provide sensory stimulation and increase hand strength.

10. Bake the crust for 7 minutes until lightly brown.

 Once again, set and pay attention to that timer.

11. Layer the sauce then the cheese and toppings onto the crust.

 Let your child unscrew the marinara jar. You may need to use hand-over-hand to help.

 Spreading sauce with the back of a spoon and picking up the small pieces of food to sprinkle is great fine motor practice. If your child likes veggies or meat, add them too.

12. Bake pizza for an additional 15 minutes.

 Again, set the kitchen timer. Hopefully your child will think that all of the waiting is worth it!

ABC Salad

Veggies & Side Dishes

Bugs On a Log

Carrot Coins

Favorite French Fries

Build-Your-Own Veggie Skewers

ABC Salad

Level I (easy)

This dish isn't so much a salad as it is a plate of crudités; however, it is another fun way to engage your child in learning while you let him play with food! I made up this recipe about a year ago when I started using the "Handwriting Without Tears" program with George, which uses a multi-sensory approach to learning letters. George loved making letters with the wooden puzzle pieces that are part of the program, so I decided to cut vegetables into long and short strips and big and small curves. I usually prep the vegetables ahead of time because I want them to be specific sizes and shapes, but as your child's fine motor and knife skills improve, he can help with this part.

Ingredients

Red, yellow, or green bell peppers (pre-cut into 3" strips and 1" strips)
Cucumbers (pre-cut into 3" strips and 1" strips)
Carrots (pre-cut into 3" strips and 1" strips)
Celery (pre-cut into 3" strips and 1" strips)
Avocado (pre-cut into curved pieces)
Tomato (pre-cut into curved pieces)
Lettuce (optional)

Tools

Knife
Cutting board

Directions

1. **Prepare the cooking area in advance. Clear all clutter. Wash and pre-cut any vegetables your child will use for his ABC Salad. Set out all ingredients and cooking utensils.**

2. **Read through the entire recipe and instructions (on the CD-ROM or print-outs) with your child, pointing to each word as you read.**

    Explain that today you are going to make letters out of vegetables! Depending on where your child is in terms of letter recognition, you may want to have an alphabet chart nearby to refer to.

3. Wash hands.

 The sensation of the water will calm and ready your child for preparing a meal. Take advantage of this time to do any last minute prep.

4. Place clean lettuce leaves on a plate.

My own children do not eat lettuce, so I skip this step so that the lettuce doesn't go to waste. We make our letters right on a plate.

5. Use the three-inch vegetable strips for long lines and the one-inch strips for short lines. The tomato and avocado slices can work as curves for such letters as C, G, B, etc.

 The first time you work on ABC Salad, try making just one letter together—perhaps the first letter in your child's name. Point to a letter on an alphabet chart or from the magnetic letters that might be on your fridge and show your child how many lines you'll need. "To make the letter E, we need one big line and three small lines."

 Select the vegetables you'll need to make the letter. "I'll use one long bell pepper and three small carrot sticks." Assemble the letter. Leave it as a model and help your child make one on his own. My kids like to spell their names out in vegetables, but it took us time to get comfortable with the process, so making an ABC Salad with one to three letters to start out is just fine!

 For children who are already spelling and reading, the possibilities are endless. You and your child can each create a short word and surprise each other with what you've written in vegetables!

Bugs On a Log

Level I (easy)

Making Bugs On a Log is a fun activity to do on a play date or for siblings to do together on a rainy day. They can get creative and use the different kinds of "bugs" to make colorful patterns. It's also an ideal midday sensory break, with all the washing, breaking, scooping, and crunching!

Don't tell the kids, but this quick, nutritious snack is a great way to get them to eat celery, which has abundant fiber and can be a gentle laxative for children who tend to get constipated.

Ingredients

Celery (approximately 1 stalk per person)
Nut butter (e.g., almond, cashew, peanut, or soy)
    (approximately 1 tablespoon per celery stalk)
Dried cranberries, raisins, currants, goji berries, etc.

Tools

Butter knife

Directions

1. **Prepare the cooking area in advance. Clear all clutter. Set out all ingredients and cooking utensils.**

2. **Read through the entire recipe and instructions (on the CD-ROM or print-outs) with your child, pointing to each word as you read.**

    Emphasize words that are specific to this recipe, like wash, scoop, and break. Connect the words to the photos as you talk about what you'll be doing.

3. **Wash hands.**

    The sensation of the water will calm and ready your child for preparing a snack. Take advantage of this time to do any last minute prep.

4. **Wash celery and break into pieces.**

    This is an excellent sensory workout! When my son is especially "rammy," I find that breaking celery stalks gives him the input that he needs to help organize his vestibular system. Have your child run the celery under cold water and then show your child how to break the ribs apart.

5. Spread nut butter onto the celery with a butter knife.

  Let your child unscrew the jar, dip a knife in, and scoop out some nut butter. You may need to use hand-over-hand to help.

 Let your child spread the nut butter onto the celery. Spreading with a knife is a wonderful way for your child to practice fine motor control. If he is enjoying spreading and is doing well with it, have your child make a "log" for you!

6. Add "bugs," making a colorful pattern.

 Picking up the small dried fruit pieces is great fine motor practice.

Count how many bugs are crawling on each log.

7. Eat and make more!

Carrot Coins

Level I (easy)

Besides green beans, carrots are the only other vegetable that my kids will eat when cooked. These carrots make a tasty side dish for fish or chicken. And washing, peeling, cutting, and smelling these carrots make for an enriching sensory experience.

Ingredients

8-10 carrots
¼ cup honey
1 teaspoon cinnamon
1 teaspoon sea salt

Yields 5-6 servings.

Tools

Peeler   Large bowl
Knife   Cutting board
Large spoon   Saucepan
Butter knife   Colander
Measuring cups   Kitchen timer
Measuring spoons

Directions

1. **Prepare the cooking area in advance. Clear all clutter. Set out all ingredients and cooking utensils.**

2. **Read through the entire recipe and instructions (on the CD-ROM or print-outs) with your child, pointing to each word as you read.**

    Emphasize words that are specific to this recipe, like peel, cut, sprinkle, etc. Connect the words to the photos as you talk about what you'll be doing.

3. **Wash hands.**

    The sensation of the water will calm and ready your child for cooking. Take advantage of this time to do any last minute prep.

4. Wash and peel the carrots.

    If your child has the strength and attention to peel a couple of carrots, that's great. Start with one and work up from there. Usually I hold the carrot and guide my son's hand with the peeler until he gets the hang of it and then he will use the peeler independently.

5. Cut carrots into round "coins."

    Use hand-over-hand with your child to cut the carrots into "coins" approximately ¼-½" thick.

6. Place carrots in a pot and cover with water.

    Your child can place the pot in the sink and turn the faucet on and off.

7. Boil carrots for 15-20 minutes until tender and then drain them into a colander.

    Once the water has come to a boil, let your child set the kitchen timer with assistance. At 15 minutes, remove one carrot with a spoon and test it for tenderness.

8. Dump carrots into a bowl. Add honey, cinnamon, and salt, and stir.

(Note: Sea salt has minerals that provide extra health benefits, but using regular table salt for this recipe is fine.)

    Your child can measure out the honey, cinnamon, and salt and dump them right into the bowl with the carrots. Squeezing honey from a "honey bear" provides deep pressure to the muscles while building strength in your child's hands (needed for writing). (Note: You can thinly coat the inside of the measuring cup with oil to allow the honey to slip out easily.) Have the dry ingredients already poured into small bowls so that your child can readily scoop them with a measuring spoon and level them off. Leveling dry ingredients off with a butter knife is great practice for fine motor skills.

    Incorporate your spices by stirring with a large spoon. Give your child time to benefit from the gross motor workout and deep pressure and scents of this sensory experience.

    Make sure to warn your child that the carrots are hot. Talk about the aroma of the cooked carrots and the cinnamon.

Give the carrots just a few minutes to cool down and then serve. If you have any left, carrot coins are yummy served cold, too.

Favorite French Fries

Level I (easy)

These fries aren't fried at all but are simply sliced and roasted in the oven with salt and olive oil. They emerge crispy and delicious and taste great on their own, or you can try adding toppings with different smells and textures like ketchup, GFCF barbeque sauce, or vinegar to expand your child's French fry repertoire. I've served these fries to grown-up company who gobble them down as quickly as my kids do.

Ingredients

7-8 medium-sized potatoes
3 tablespoons olive oil
2 teaspoons sea salt

Yields 4-5 servings.

Tools

Large spoon or tongs	Measuring spoons
Butter knife	Colander
Knife	Cutting board
Spatula	Baking sheet
Vegetable brush	Kitchen timer

Directions

1. **Prepare the cooking area in advance. Clear all clutter. Set out all ingredients and cooking utensils.**

2. **Read through the entire recipe and instructions (on the CD-ROM or print-outs) with your child, pointing to each word as you read.**

    Emphasize words and phrases that repeat, like cut, tablespoon, set the timer, etc. Connect the words to the photos as you talk about what you'll be doing.

3. **Wash hands.**

    The sensation of the water will calm and ready your child for cooking. Take advantage of this time to do any last minute prep.

4. Preheat the oven to 400°.

 Let your child set the temperature with your assistance. Say the numbers aloud as you do this.

5. Wash the potatoes.

 Count how many potatoes you have. As you count them, place the potatoes in a colander in the sink. When all of the potatoes are in, turn on the cold water and let it run over the potatoes. Pick up each one—and count it as you do—and scrub with a vegetable brush or scrubber. Rinse the potatoes one more time (and why not count them one more time?)

6. Cut the potatoes into bite-sized pieces.

 Use hand-over-hand with your child to cut the potatoes in half, then in quarters, then in quarters again. They don't have to be sliced at any special thickness and don't worry if they're not even.

7. Place potatoes on a baking sheet.

 I like to use simple tasks like this one to highlight prepositions. I'll repeat a chant like "On the sheet…on the sheet…on the sheet…" to direct my son's attention while he places the potatoes on the baking sheet independently.

8. Drizzle olive oil over the potatoes and dust with salt.

(Note: Sea salt has minerals that provide extra health benefits, but using regular table salt for this recipe is fine.)

 Help your child to measure the olive oil and to slowly pour it over the potatoes. Help him measure the salt and level it off with a butter knife before sprinkling it over the potatoes. Let him use a large spoon or tongs to toss the potatoes, making sure that they are evenly coated in oil and salt.

9. Bake 20 minutes, then turn over the fries with a spatula and bake for another 20 minutes.

 Let your child set the kitchen timer with assistance. When it rings at 20 minutes, take the baking sheet out of the oven and flip fries with a spatula. Return to the oven and let your child set the timer again for 20 minutes. The fries should get crispy and brown on both sides.

Build-Your-Own Veggie Skewers

Level I (easy)

Fruit skewers are fun to build with children, but since I find that veggies are harder to get my kids to eat, I save the skewering fun for veggies. Use any combination of vegetables that are easy to poke through a skewer. You can work on patterns as you build your skewers, as well as basic counting. How many vegetables can you get on one skewer?

Ingredients

Black olives
Cherry tomatoes
Cucumber slices
Avocado slices
Pickle slices

Tools

Knife
Can opener
Skewers
Small bowls for each vegetable
Cutting board
Colander

Directions

1. **Prepare the cooking area in advance. Clear all clutter. Set out all ingredients and cooking utensils.**

2. **Read through the entire recipe and instructions (on the CD-ROM or print-outs) with your child, pointing to each word as you read.**
    Emphasize words that repeat, like wash, cut, dump, etc. Connect the words to the photos as you talk about what you'll be doing.

3. **Wash hands.**
    The sensation of the water will calm and ready your child for preparing a snack. Take advantage of this time to do any last minute prep.

4. **Open the can of black olives, rinse them in a colander under cold water, and drain them.**

   Remove the lid yourself, as the edges will be sharp, and allow your child to dump the olives into a colander in the sink and turn on the cold water. Then have your child dump the rinsed black olives into a bowl.

5. **Wash the cherry tomatoes under cold water.**

   Guide your child to turn on the cold water and let run over the tomatoes. Turn off water and place the tomatoes in a bowl.

6. **Wash and chop the cucumber.**

   Use hand-over-hand with your child and cut the cucumber into round circles.

   (Note: if you are not using an organic cucumber, I recommend peeling before using.) Put the cucumber rounds into a bowl.

7. **Peel and slice the avocado and put into a bowl.**

   I think that avocados are really challenging for a child to cut. I generally have the kids watch or will do hand-over-hand with them after I've already cut the avocado in half and removed the pit.

   If avocados are new foods to your child, take some time to examine its bumpy skin and slimy interior. Point out that an avocado has a shell on the outside and a pit in the middle. What other vegetables or fruits do you know that have a shell on the outside? A pit on the inside?

8. **Open the pickle jar and put some slices into a bowl.**

   Opening a jar is a good gross motor challenge. If it's a brand new jar, you can get it started and then hand it off to your child to finish.

9. **Make your skewers.**

    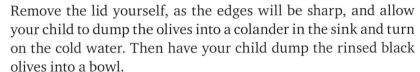
   Model to your child how to put a piece of vegetable onto the skewer. As he becomes comfortable with the activity, you can have fun making patterns: avocado-tomato-pickle-avocado-tomato-pickle, and so on. Comment on the colors of the different vegetables that you are using. Make skewers for everyone in the family. Eat right away or put on a platter and save for dinner time.

Banana Pops

Banana Chocolate
Chip Bread

Snacks & Treats

Tasty Trail Mix

Carob-Coconut
Cookies

Lemonade

Fruity Smoothies

Apple Hamantashen

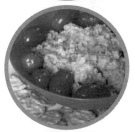

Yummy Hummus

Crispy Rice Squares

Banana Pops

Level I (easy)

These "popsicles" are much more nutritious than the typical popsicles that come out of a box—plus they're really fun to make and eat! There's lots of stuff to do with your hands in this recipe—so it's a good one for working on fine motor skills. The possibilities for variety are endless. This is a good recipe to start with for novice chefs.

Ingredients

    1 banana per person
    Honey
    Cinnamon
    GFCF granola

Tools

    Aluminum foil

Directions

1. **Prepare the cooking area in advance. Clear all clutter. Set out all ingredients and cooking utensils.**

2. **Read through the entire recipe and instructions (on the CD-ROM or print-outs) with your child, pointing to each word as you read.**

   Emphasize words that are specific to this recipe, like peel, sprinkle, wrap, etc. Connect the words to the photos as you talk about what you'll be doing.

3. **Wash hands.**

   The sensation of the water will calm and ready your child for preparing a snack. Take advantage of this time to do any last minute prep.

4. **Roll out a small sheet of foil.**

   Look at your banana's width and length and guesstimate together how much foil you'll need.

5. **Peel the banana and place on the foil sheet.**
   You might need to help get the banana started but then encourage your child to peel on his own. [Tip: For those whose kids are

tactilely defensive, if you cut a bit off the bottom of the banana and start peeling from that end, you won't be left with any of those sticky, stringy things!)

6. Cover the banana with the toppings of your child's choice.

   Offer your child choices: honey, cinnamon, granola, chocolate chips, raisins, chopped nuts. Use gesture and language and allow your child to make choices. Help him squeeze honey, sprinkle cinnamon and granola or other toppings according to his requests.

7. Wrap the foil around the banana.

Make sure that the whole banana is covered in foil to avoid freezer burn.

8. Place in the freezer.

Banana Pops need 12-24 hours to freeze. Write yourself a note, reminding you to eat the banana pops! When they are ready, you simply unwrap the foil and eat as you would a popsicle.

For more variation, try putting your frozen bananas into a blender sometime. Add a little honey and you will make a delicious vegan "ice cream!"

Tasty Trail Mix

Level I (easy)

Trail mix is a fun way to compare tastes and textures. Here is one recipe to get you started, but you and your family can create any variety that you like: add your favorite dried fruits and nuts, cereals, and spices. This is currently our favorite version because it's got chocolate in it! Tasty Trail Mix requires only measuring, pouring, and stirring, so this is a great recipe to begin your cooking adventures.

Ingredients

2 cups pretzels
2 cups GFCF cereal
2 cups GFCF chocolate chips
2 cups raisins
2 cups nuts

Yields 10 servings.

Tools

Large spoon
Measuring cups
Large bowl
Small bowl
Airtight container or zip top plastic bag

Directions

1. **Prepare the cooking area in advance. Clear all clutter. Set out all ingredients and cooking utensils.**

2. **Read through the entire recipe and instructions (on the CD-ROM or print-outs) with your child, pointing to each word as you read.**

    Emphasize words that repeat, like cup, pour, mix, etc. Connect the words to the photos as you talk about what you'll be doing.

3. **Wash hands.**

    The sensation of the water will calm and ready your child for preparing a snack. Take advantage of this time to do any last minute prep.

4. Measure out all ingredients and dump into a large bowl.

   Since the recipe calls for 2 cups of each ingredient, there is a lot of simple math that you can do here. How many cups of pretzels are in the bowl? How many cups of pretzels and cereal are in the bowl? How many cups of ingredients will be in the bowl when we're finished making the trail mix?

5. Stir the mixture with a big spoon.

 Since it doesn't really matter that things are mixed evenly in this recipe, this is a great place to practice the skill of stirring. If your child prefers, mixing with clean hands is an opportunity for some sensory input. Let your child stir as long as it keeps his interest.

6. Pour into a bowl what you want to eat at the moment and put the rest in an airtight container or plastic storage bag.

Pouring the mix is great for developing gross motor skills but might require hand-over-hand guidance.

I like to keep a bag of trail mix in the car in case we get stuck in traffic and need a quick, non-messy snack. The nuts and raisins add protein and fiber to hold hungry kids over until the next meal.

Lemonade

Level 1 (easy)

I'll bet your children will enjoy making lemonade as a special treat on a hot day as much as mine do! This is a good recipe to make during a play date. Why not set up a lemonade stand in front of the house? It presents a great opportunity to interact with neighbors and practice social skills. And making change is a meaningful way to practice emerging math skills.

We make our lemonade with a stevia-based sweetener, which is natural and wonderfully sweet. Note: a small amount of stevia yields a sweet lemonade! If you plan to use sugar instead, you will need 1½ cups sugar.

Ingredients

4 cups cold water
5-6 lemons
2 teaspoons stevia liquid concentrate
Ice cubes

Yields 4-6 servings.

Tools

Long handled spoon   Juicer
Knife   Cutting board
Measuring spoons   Pitcher
Measuring cups   Small bowl

Directions

1. **Prepare the cooking area in advance. Clear all clutter. Set out all ingredients and cooking utensils.**

2. **Read through the entire recipe and instructions (on the CD-ROM or print-outs) with your child, pointing to each word as you read.**
    Emphasize words that repeat, like measure, pour, squeeze, etc. Connect the words to the photos as you talk about what you'll be doing.

3. **Wash hands.**
    The sensation of the water will calm and ready your child for preparing a treat. Take advantage of this time to do any last minute prep.

4. Measure cold water and pour into a pitcher.

 Your child can fill the measuring cup right from the sink and pour into a big pitcher.

5. Juice the lemons and add to the pitcher.

 Count your lemons! Use hand-over-hand to help your child cut the lemons in half and then juice them into a small bowl. Practice fine motor control by picking out any seeds that get in. Pour the lemon juice into the pitcher.

6. Measure and pour in the stevia, then stir.

 Stevia comes in a dropper, which requires fine motor control, and is fun for children to squirt into the measuring spoon! Stirring with a long spoon provides great input to the upper body.

7. Add ice cubes to a glass and pour in some lemonade.

 Dumping ice cubes from a tray is a good gross motor activity. Put the cubes in a glass, pour a small amount of lemonade into it, and taste it with your child. Is it cold enough? Or does it need more ice cubes? Does it taste sweet or sour? There are lots of great vocabulary words to use with lemonade!

8. Bonus Step: Lemonade Stand

 Doing an old-fashioned lemonade stand is a great opportunity for learning! Make a colorful sign advertising your sale items and prices. (You can use markers or cut out letters and pictures from old magazines.) Charge 25 cents a cup and play with different combinations of coins to equal 25 cents. Practice greeting the neighbors who will come to the stand, using words or pictures according to your child's ability.

Fruity Smoothies

Level I (easy)

My kids looove using the blender. There's something so satisfying about putting stuff into a machine, pushing a button, and having it come out in a different form! Making smoothies is a sensory adventure: from peeling mushy bananas to squeezing honey from a bottle to handling frozen ice cubes. Keep in mind that some children with auditory defensiveness may react strongly to the sound of the blender.

If you are new to cooking with your child, this is a great recipe to start with. It mostly involves measuring and pouring and you'll come out with a great smoothie even if the measuring isn't precise. You can always add more fruit, juice, etc. after you taste.

Ingredients

2 cups frozen mixed berries
½ cup milk or milk substitute (e.g., almond, rice, or soy)
1 cup orange juice
1 banana
1 tablespoon honey (optional)
1 tablespoon flax oil (optional)
3-4 ice cubes

Yields enough smoothie to fill 1 tall glass or 2 juice glasses.

Tools

Measuring cups
Measuring spoons
Blender

Directions

1. **Prepare the cooking area in advance. Clear all clutter. Set out all ingredients and cooking utensils.**

2. **Read through the entire recipe and instructions (on the CD-ROM or printouts) with your child, pointing to each word as you read.**

    Emphasize words that repeat, like cup, tablespoon, pour, etc. Connect the words to the photos as you talk about what you'll be doing.

3. Wash hands.

 The sensation of the water will calm and ready your child for preparing a snack. Take advantage of this time to do any last minute prep.

4. Measure each ingredient one by one and dump them into blender.

 Provide hand-over-hand help with deep pressure to assist your child in pouring the liquids. You can also pour the juice and milk into smaller pitchers ahead of time that are easier to pour from.

 You might need to help get the banana started but then encourage your child to peel on his own. [Tip: For those whose kids are tactilely defensive, if you cut a bit off the bottom of the banana and start peeling from that end, you won't be left with any of those sticky, stringy things!]

 Squeezing honey from a "honey bear" is a fun way to pour out the honey and it provides deep pressure to the muscles while building strength in your child's hands (needed for writing).

 Dumping ice cubes from a tray is a good gross motor activity and picking up and handling ice cubes provides a fun sensory experience and tricky fine motor skill work!

5. Blend on "puree" setting for 1-2 minutes until berries and ice are crushed and smoothie is smooth.

 What kid do you know who doesn't like pushing buttons? Point to the puree button on the blender and let your child push to his heart's content. If your child is sensitive to loud noises, you may want to take him into another room while you use the blender. Give your child a warning before you turn the blender on. Cover your ears and say "Loud" and gesture to the blender.

6. Pour into a glass—enjoy!

 I like to fill a juice glass for each of us and clink glasses with my kids. We toast to a great day, time together, or simply l'chaim!, "To life!"

Yummy Hummus

Level I (easy)

Hummus with veggies and rice crackers is a popular snack or even light lunch in our house. Hummus is much cheaper to make on your own than buying it pre-made and it's quick and easy. I usually double this recipe for my hungry crew.

This recipe gives your child lots of opportunities for fine motor practice—from dumping chickpeas, measuring tahini and olive oil, to peeling garlic and squeezing lemons. You can also have lots of fun experimenting with different things to chop up and dip into the hummus—from baby carrots and olives to broccoli florets and cucumber wedges.

Ingredients

1 16-ounce can chickpeas
2 tablespoons tahini
2 tablespoons olive oil
1 teaspoon sea salt
1-2 garlic cloves
1 lemon
1 teaspoon cumin (optional)

Yields 4-6 servings.

Tools

Knife   Juicer
Butter knife   Small bowl
Large spoon   Cutting board
Measuring spoons   Colander
Can opener   Blender or food processor

Directions

1. **Prepare the cooking area in advance. Clear all clutter. Set out all ingredients and cooking utensils.**

2. **Read through the entire recipe and instructions (on the CD-ROM or print-outs) with your child, pointing to each word as you read.**

    Emphasize words that repeat, like tablespoon, squeeze, pour, etc. Connect the words to the photos as you talk about what you'll be doing.

3. Wash hands.

The sensation of the water will calm and ready your child for preparing a snack. Take advantage of this time to do any last minute prep.

4. Open the can of chickpeas, rinse them in a colander under cold water, drain them, and put them into the blender.

Remove the lid yourself, as the edges will be sharp, and allow your child to dump the chickpeas into a colander in the sink and turn on the cold water. Then have your child dump the rinsed chickpeas into the blender.

5. Add tahini, olive oil, salt, and garlic to the blender.

(Note: Sea salt has minerals that provide extra health benefits, but using regular table salt for this recipe is fine.)

If necessary, help your child to measure out the tahini, olive oil, and salt. Have your salt already poured into a small bowl (with a lid for storage) so your child can readily scoop it with a measuring spoon. Leveling dry ingredients off with a butter knife is great practice for fine motor skills. Taking the peel off of the garlic is great practice for fine motor skills too, but can be a frustrating job, so stand by to give help.

6. Juice the lemon and add to the chickpea mixture.

Use hand-over-hand to help your child cut the lemon in half and then juice it straight into the blender. Make sure that no seeds get in. Squeezing a juicer is great sensory and gross motor work!

7. Add any additional spices that your family likes, such as cumin, and blend on "puree" setting for 1-2 minutes until smooth and creamy.

What kid do you know who doesn't like pushing buttons? Point to the puree button on the blender and let your child push to his heart's content. If your child is sensitive to loud noises, you may want to take him into another room while you use the blender. Give your child a warning before you turn the blender on. Cover your ears and say "Loud" and gesture to the blender.

After blending, if the hummus seems too thick or stiff for dipping, add another tablespoon of olive oil and puree again.

8. Spoon the hummus out of the blender and into a serving bowl.

Your child can help you lay out crackers and veggies, like baby carrots and bell pepper strips, to dip with.

Crispy Rice Squares

Level I (easy)

Making these treats is a good play date activity. The kids will get to experience lots of sensory input including greasy butter, sticky marshmallows, and the crispy crunch of the final product.

Although Kellogg's Rice Krispies™ cereal is not gluten-free, there are plenty of gluten-free brown rice cereals that you can use for this classic recipe. Nature's Path Koala Crisp™ is the current favorite in my house. I've made this recipe to take into George's class, where most kids aren't on gluten-free diets, and the kids gobbled them down just the same.

Ingredients

12 tablespoons (1½ sticks) butter or vegan butter substitute
    + 1 tablespoon for greasing baking pan
1 10-ounce package marshmallows
1 teaspoon vanilla extract
1 10-ounce box GF brown rice cereal

Yields 12-15 squares.

Tools

Knife
Wooden spoon
Measuring spoons
Saucepan
Baking dish (13" x 9")
Kitchen timer

Directions

1. **Prepare the cooking area in advance. Clear all clutter. Set out all ingredients and cooking utensils.**

2. **Read through the entire recipe and instructions (on the CD-ROM or print-outs) with your child, pointing to each word as you read.**

    Emphasize words that repeat, like "pour, then stir…pour, then stir…." Connect the words to the photos as you talk about what you'll be doing.

3. Wash hands.

 The sensation of the water will calm and ready your child for cooking. Take advantage of this time to do any last minute prep.

4. Grease the baking dish with butter or butter substitute.

 Give your child a pat of butter [or shortening of your choice] and let him go to town spreading it all over the baking dish.

5. Melt the butter (or substitute) and marshmallows in saucepan over low heat.

 Help your child measure out the butter, whether in sticks or from a tub.

 Your child can watch you from a safe distance as you melt the butter over low heat and then stir in the marshmallows until melted and combined. Point out to your child how the butter and marshmallows are changing form from solid to liquid. When the marshmallows are melted down, take the pan off of the hot burner and set on a cool one.

6. Stir vanilla extract into the butter and marshmallow mixture.

Use hand-over-hand to help your child measure and pour the vanilla extract into the butter-marshmallow mixture. Give your child time to benefit from the gross motor workout and deep pressure sensory experience of stirring this thick mixture with a wooden spoon.

7. Pour the cereal into the marshmallow mixture.

Help your child to pour the cereal in slowly. Pour about ⅓ of the box then stop and stir well. Pour another ⅓, stir; pour the final ⅓ and stir until the cereal is evenly coated with the butter-marshmallow mixture. This is a great upper body workout!

8. Pour the mixture into the baking dish and press flat with the back of a spoon.

 (If the saucepan is still hot, the adult ought to do the pouring.) This is a fun step! Offer your child a spoon and help him press down the mixture and make it even across the baking dish.

9. Let cool down and cut into squares.

Make sure to get one for yourself—these treats don't last long in my house!

Banana Chocolate Chip Bread

Level II (moderately difficult)

When the bananas in your fruit bowl become a little bit mushy, it's the perfect time to make banana bread! Adding GFCF chocolate chips into the batter makes this into more of a sweet treat than a bread—ideal for a special snack or even dessert.

The resistance created by mashing soft bananas with a fork gives nice sensory input. This recipe also features a number of steps that help to develop fine motor skills, such as peeling the bananas and taking soft butter out of its paper.

Ingredients

8 tablespoons (1 stick) butter or vegan butter substitute (softened), plus 1 tablespoon for greasing loaf pan
½ cup honey
2 eggs
2 teaspoons vanilla extract
3 large ripe bananas
2 cups rice flour
1 teaspoon baking soda
1 cup GFCF chocolate chips

Yields 10-12 slices.

Tools

2 Large bowls	Measuring spoons
2 Medium-sized bowls	Loaf pan (5" x 9")
2 Large spoons	Paper towel
Fork	Toothpicks
Butter knife	Kitchen timer
Measuring cups	

Directions

1. **Prepare the cooking area in advance. Clear all clutter. Set out all ingredients and cooking utensils.**

2. **Read through the entire recipe and instructions (on the CD-ROM or print-outs) with your child, pointing to each word as you read.**

    Emphasize words that are specific to this recipe like peel, mash, mix, etc. Connect the words to the photos as you talk about what you'll be doing.

3. **Wash hands.**

    The sensation of the water will calm and ready your child for cooking. Take advantage of this time to do any last minute prep.

4. **Preheat the oven to 325°.**

    Let your child set the temperature with your assistance. Say the numbers aloud as you do this.

5. **Combine the butter and honey in a large bowl.**

      Help your child take the softened butter out of its paper and mash it with a large spoon in a large bowl until smooth.

    Have your child squeeze the honey from the "honey bear" into the measuring cup. The harder it is to do, the more coordination it will require and the greater deep pressure it will provide his sensory system while building strength in his hands (needed for writing). Have him pour the honey into the bowl with the butter. (Note: You can thinly coat the inside of the measuring cup with oil to allow the honey to slip out easily.)

6. **Add eggs and vanilla extract to the honey-butter combo.**

    Have your child crack the eggs at the bottom of a medium-sized bowl. Let him punch them, stick his thumbs into them, etc. There is no wrong way to do this and he will choose the method that provides the type of sensory input he is seeking.

    Have your child pick out the broken eggshell pieces and wipe them onto a paper towel. Then direct him to wash his hands. These activities provide excellent fine motor skill practice.

    Once all eggshell pieces are removed, have him pour the eggs into the honey-butter bowl.

    Provide hand-over-hand help with deep pressure to assist your child in pouring the vanilla extract into the measuring spoon and pouring into the honey-butter bowl.

7. Mix the wet ingredients together in the big bowl.

 Have your child steady the bowl on the counter with one arm and stir with the other. This helps build strength and coordination while providing deep pressure to his joints and muscles.

8. Peel and mash the bananas in a medium-sized bowl then add them to the honey-butter combo.

 Open the first banana and start to peel it. Holding the banana, show your child how to pull the peel down. Start to peel the next section, then offer the peel to your child to pull down. When the peel is completely off, place the banana in a medium-sized bowl. Continue with the next two bananas, allowing your child to practice peeling as independently as he is able. Your holding the banana can stabilize it and allow him to focus his attention on the work of peeling.

 When the bananas are all peeled, take a fork and press down to smash the bananas. Place the fork in your child's hand and with hand-over-hand guidance, help him to move the fork up and down into the banana. The resistance of the fork into the banana provides nice sensory input.

 When the mashing is complete, your child can pick up the bowl and dump into the honey-butter bowl. He can mix the mashed bananas into the wet mixture with a large spoon.

 Practice counting slowly to 10 (or 20 if your child is able) for each time your child stirs the mixture. If your child gets tired along the way, that's fine! Just say, "My turn!," pick up the spoon, and finish counting.

9. Combine all of the dry ingredients in a clean, big bowl.

  Allow your child to scoop the rice flour (with clean hands) into the measuring cup and level it off with a butter knife before dumping it into a large bowl. Have your baking soda already poured into a small bowl so that your child can readily scoop it with a measuring spoon. Leveling dry ingredients off with a butter knife is great practice for fine motor skills.

 Have 1 cup of chocolate chips ready for your child to pour in. (Note: Carob chips or raisins can be substituted.) I always have these premeasured so George isn't tempted to reach into the bag of chocolate chips and help himself. If chocolate is a rare treat for your child, have a few chips set aside for him. You can practice counting, "We can taste 1-2-3-4-5 chips now, but we'll have more chips later when we taste them in the bread!"

10. Slowly pour the dry ingredients into the wet mixture.

 You can trade roles with your child as you cook together and repeat favorite recipes. You may have your child hold the bowl while you use a spoon to pour out the dry ingredients. The next time you make Banana Chocolate Chip Bread, you can hold the bowl and offer the spoon to your child. Trading roles creates variations so that cooking together is a dynamic process that will encourage your child to pay attention to what is happening moment to moment.

11. Pour the batter into a greased 5" x 9" loaf pan and level it out.

 Give your child a pat of butter (or shortening of your choice) and let him go to town rubbing the butter inside the loaf pan (check to make sure that the corners get coverage).

  Help your child hold the bowl and pour the batter into the loaf pan. Show him that the batter needs to be evened out across the pan with a spoon in order to bake correctly.

12. Bake at 325° for up to 1 hour.

  Assist your child in setting the kitchen timer for 45 minutes. Check the bread at that point to make sure that it's not burning.

  When you take the bread out of the oven, invite your child to watch as you stick a toothpick in the middle of the bread. If it comes out moist, the bread needs some more time to bake. You can point out the difference between the words wet and dry: "The toothpick comes out dry when I stick it in the ends of the bread...but look at how wet it is when I poke it in the middle." The bread may take a full hour to bake.

 Let the bread cool down before cutting a piece for both of you to enjoy!

Carob-Coconut Cookies

Level II (moderately difficult)

Because the ingredients in this recipe have odd-ball textures (flour, coconut flakes, honey, eggs), this is a particularly good recipe to try with a child who experiences tactile defensiveness. Initially, he may resist touching these ingredients, but with repeated exposure and the incentive of eating the finished product, eventually your kid will join in the fun. Only carry out as many of the suggestions below as you and your child can handle. Take a deep breath, let him make a mess, look for opportunities for learning, and enjoy the process!

Ingredients

    1 cup almond flour
    1 cup unsweetened coconut flakes
    ½ cup carob powder
    1 teaspoon cinnamon
    1 teaspoon baking powder
    1 teaspoon salt
    2 eggs
    8 tablespoons butter or vegan butter substitute (melted)
        plus 2 tablespoons for greasing baking sheets
    ½ cup honey
    1 teaspoon vanilla extract

    Yields 12-15 cookies.

Tools

Butter knife	1 Medium-sized bowl
Large spoon	1 Small microwave-safe bowl
Spatula	2 Baking sheets
Measuring spoons	Paper towel
Measuring cups	Kitchen timer
1 Large bowl	

Directions

1. **Prepare the cooking area in advance. Clear all clutter. Set out all ingredients and cooking utensils.**

2. **Read through the entire recipe and instructions (on the CD-ROM or print-outs) with your child, pointing to each word as you read.**

Emphasize words that repeat, like measure, pour, mix, etc. Connect the words to the photos as you talk about what you'll be doing.

3. **Wash hands.**

The sensation of the water will calm and ready your child for cooking. Take advantage of this time to do any last minute prep.

4. **Preheat the oven to 350°.**

Let your child set the temperature with your assistance. Say the numbers aloud as you do this.

5. **Mix all of the dry ingredients in a large bowl.**

Point to the number amount for each ingredient and say it aloud to encourage number recognition. Ask your child if he added "more" or "less" almond flour than carob powder?

Allow your child to scoop the dry ingredients (with clean hands) into the measuring devices and level them off before dumping them into a large bowl. Have your cinnamon, baking powder, and salt already poured into small bowls (with lids for storage) so your child can readily scoop them with measuring spoons. Leveling dry ingredients off with a butter knife is great practice for fine motor skills.

6. **Add the eggs, melted butter (or substitute), honey, and vanilla extract to the dry ingredients and mix to combine.**

Have your child crack the eggs at the bottom of a medium-sized bowl. Let him punch them, stick his thumbs into them, etc. There is no wrong way to do this and he will choose the method that provides the type of sensory input he is seeking.

Have your child pick out the broken eggshell pieces and wipe them onto a paper towel. Then direct him to wash his hands. These activities provide excellent fine motor skill practice.

Help your child develop number sense and dexterity by letting him push the buttons on the microwave to melt the butter in a microwave safe dish. Remember to let the dish cool off before asking him to pour the butter into the bowl of dry ingredients.

 Have your child squeeze the honey from the "honey bear" into the measuring cup. The harder it is to do, the more co-ordination it will require and the greater deep pressure it will provide his sensory system while building strength in his hands (needed for writing). (Note: You can thinly coat the inside of the measuring cup with oil to allow the honey to slip out easily.)

 Provide hand-over-hand help with deep pressure to assist your child in pouring the vanilla extract into the measuring spoon.

 Mixing thick ingredients in a large bowl is an excellent source of deep pressure and gross and fine motor skill development. Rhythmically chant "Stirring, stirring, stirring…" and pause periodically to see if your child will chime in.

7. Drop batter by spoonfuls onto a greased baking sheet.

 Give your child a pat of butter [or shortening of your choice] and let him go to town spreading it all over the baking sheet.

 Help your child measure out spoonfuls of the batter with hand-over-hand assistance, if necessary. Visually show him how to space out the cookies so they won't melt together.

8. Bake at 350° for 10-15 minutes.

 Let your child set the kitchen timer with assistance.

9. Remove cooled cookies from baking sheet.

 This is another opportunity to work on fine motor skills. Remember: broken cookies taste just as good as whole ones.

Apple Hamantashen

Level III (more difficult)

Hamantashen are the traditional triangle-shaped cookies eaten during the Jewish holiday of Purim. My son went to Jewish preschool and I didn't want him to be left out of the Purim festivities so I developed this gluten-free recipe that we've made together for the last three years. We like using applesauce for the filling, but you could use any favorite jam or jelly, chocolate chips, nut butter, etc.

Because the dough needs to be refrigerated for several hours, we usually make the dough before bedtime and wake up and form and bake the cookies in the morning. The heavy work of mashing, stirring, pouring, and smushing provides soothing deep pressure to the large muscles of George's trunk and really wakes up his sensory system.

Ingredients

8 tablespoons (1 stick) butter or vegan butter substitute (softened)
    plus 1 tablespoon for greasing baking sheet
1 cup honey
3 eggs
½ cup orange juice
1 teaspoon vanilla extract
4 cups GF flour
1 teaspoon xanthan gum
1 teaspoon baking powder
1 teaspoon salt
Applesauce, approximately ¼-½ cup

Yields 12-15 cookies.

Tools

3 Large spoons	2 Large bowls
Butter knife	1 Medium-sized bowl
Spatula	2 Baking sheets
Measuring cups	Paper towel
Measuring spoons	Kitchen timer

Directions

1. **Prepare the cooking area in advance. Clear all clutter. Set out all ingredients and cooking utensils.**

2. **Read through the entire recipe and instructions (on the CD-ROM or print-outs) with your child, pointing to each word as you read.**

Emphasize words that repeat, like scoop, "level it off," flatten, etc. Connect the words to the photos as you talk about what you'll be doing.

3. **Wash hands.**

The sensation of the water will calm and ready your child for cooking. Take advantage of this time to do any last minute prep.

4. **Mix butter (or substitute), honey, eggs, juice, and vanilla in a large bowl until well blended.**

Have your child use a large spoon to mash the softened butter. This works the large muscles of the trunk and provides soothing deep pressure to the sensory system. Likewise, squeezing the honey from the bottle into the measuring cup provides deep pressure and promotes coordination. (Note: You can thinly coat the inside of the measuring cup with oil to allow the honey to slip out easily.)

Have your child crack the eggs at the bottom of a medium-sized bowl. Let him punch them, stick his thumbs into them, etc. There is no wrong way to do this and he will choose the method that provides the type of sensory input he is seeking.

Have your child pick out the broken eggshell pieces and wipe them onto a paper towel. Then direct him to wash his hands. These activities provide excellent fine motor skill practice.

Provide hand-over-hand help with deep pressure to assist your child in pouring the vanilla extract into the measuring spoon and the orange juice into a cup.

Mixing thick ingredients in a large bowl is an excellent source of deep pressure and gross and fine motor skill development. Rhythmically chant "Stirring, stirring, stirring…" and pause periodically to see if your child will chime in.

5. **Mix dry ingredients in another big bowl.**

Have your xanthan gum, baking powder, and salt already poured into small bowls (with lids for storage) so your child can readily scoop them with measuring spoons. Leveling dry ingredients off with a butter knife is great practice for fine motor skills.

6. **Slowly pour the dry ingredients into the wet ingredients and stir until blended.**

    Use hand-over-hand guidance to help your child pour the dry ingredients into the bowl of wet ingredients. Then have your child steady the bowl on the counter with one arm and stir the mixture with the other. This helps build strength and coordination while providing deep pressure to his joints and muscles.

7. **Refrigerate the batter for 2-3 hours (or overnight is okay).**

    Have your child set the kitchen timer with assistance. Say the numbers out loud and talk about how many minutes are in an hour.

8. **Preheat oven to 350°.**

    Let your child set the temperature with your assistance. Say the numbers aloud as you do this.

9. **Roll small balls of dough and place on a cookie sheet. Flatten them with the palms of your hands and then form into triangles.**

    As with making meatballs, rolling dough is a fun sensory activity. Model for your child how to flatten the balls with the palm of your hand.

    Work together using hand-over-hand guidance to pinch the dough into triangles. You can use a block, magnet, or picture of a triangle as a reference for your child and count to three as you fold the three sides. We never go for perfect bakery form.

10. **Place a small dab of applesauce into the center of the dough triangles.**

     Opening the jar of applesauce is great gross motor practice. And dipping the spoon into the applesauce and spooning it onto the Hamantshen makes great fine motor practice.

11. **Bake for 20 minutes.**

     Let your child set the kitchen timer with assistance. Say the numbers aloud as you do this.

12. **Remove cooled Hamantashen from baking sheet. Garnish with some dried fruit and nuts if you like.**

    It is a tradition to give small packages of baked goods and treats to friends and neighbors at Purim time. You can make baggies filled with these Hamantashen and attach a picture that your child drew and share them with friends, teachers, therapists, grandparents, etc.

Resources
for Parents, Teachers & Kids

Websites

Diets

- *Body Ecology: 7 Principles System of Healing*
  www.bodyecologydiet.com
  > This website provides information about the Body Ecology Diet™.

- *Breaking the Vicious Cycle: The Specific Carbohydrate Diet™*
  www.breakingtheviciouscycle.info
  > This website provides information about the Specific Carbohydrate Diet.

- *Celiac.com: Celiac Disease and Gluten-free Diet Information Since 1995*
  www.celiac.com
  > This website provides information and resources about celiac disease and the gluten-free diet.

- *Glutenfree.com*
  http://www.glutenfree.com/index.cfm/autisminformation
  > This site provides recipes and links for gluten-free shopping.

- *Healing Thresholds: Connecting Community and Science to Heal Autism*
  http://autism.healingthresholds.com/therapy/casein-free-diet
     This site provides helpful advice and scientific information about the GFCF diet.

- *Talk about Curing Autism*
  http://gfcf-diet.talkaboutcuringautism.org
     This is the website that I used to get started on the GFCF diet. It contains a wealth of information and helpful resources, including a ten-week plan for getting started. Highly recommended!

Free Clipart

- *All Free Original Clipart*
  www.free-graphics.com

- *Clipart Castle*
  www.clipartcastle.com

- *Free Clipart pictures*
  www.freeclipartpictures.com

Books for Parents & Teachers

A Picture's Worth: PECS and Other Visual Communication Strategies in Autism by Andy Bondy and Lori Frost. Woodbine House (2002).

Autism 24/7: A Family Guide to Learning at Home and in the Community by Andy Bondy and Lori Frost. Woodbine House (2007).

Eating Gluten-Free with Emily: A Story for Children with Celiac Disease by Bonnie Kruszka. BookSurge Publishing (2009).

The GF Kid: A Celiac Disease Survival Guide by Melissa London. Woodbine House (2005).

Gluten-Free Kids: Raising Happy, Healthy Children with Celiac Disease, Autism, and Other Conditions by Danna Korn. Woodbine House (2010).

Incredible Edible Gluten-Free Food for Kids: 150 Family-Tested Recipes by Sheri Sanderson. Woodbine House (2002).

Letters to Sam: A Grandfather's Lessons on Love, Loss, and the Gifts of Life by Dan Gottlieb. Sterling (2008).

Mixed Signals: Understanding and Treating Your Child's Sensory Processing Issues by Mary Lashno. Woodbine House (2010).

The Out-of-Sync Child: Recognizing and Coping with Sensory Processing Disorder by Carol Kranowitz. Perigee Trade (2006).

Reaching Out, Joining In: Teaching Social Skills to Young Children with Autism by Mary Jane Weiss and Sandra Harris. Woodbine House (2001).

Relationship Development Intervention for Children, Adolescents and Adults by Dr. Steven Gutstein and Rachelle Sheely. Jessica Kingsley Publishers (2002).

Relationship Development Intervention with Young Children: Social and Emotional Development Activities for Asperger Syndrome, Autism, PDD and NLD by Dr. Steven Gutstein and Rachelle Sheely. Jessica Kingsley Publishers (2002).

Seeing is Believing: Video Self-Modeling for People with Autism and Other Developmental Disabilities by Tom Buggey. Woodbine House (2009).

Self-Help Skills for People with Autism: A Systematic Teaching Approach by Stephen Anderson, Amy Jablonski, Marcus Thomeer, and Vicki Madaus Knapp. Woodbine House (2007).

Special Children, Challenged Parents: The Struggles and Rewards of Raising a Child with a Disability by Dr. Robert Naseef. Brookes Publishing Company (2001).

Teaching by Design: Using Your Computer to Create Materials for Students with Learning Differences by Kimberly Voss. Woodbine House (2005).

Visual Supports for People with Autism: A Guide for Parents and Professionals by Marlene Cohen and Donna Sloan. Woodbine House (2007).

The Wisdom of Sam: Observations on Life from an Uncommon Child by Dan Gottlieb. Hay House (2010)

Books About Food for Children:

Reading about food and cooking is a wonderful way to enhance your cooking experiences with your kids! Some of our favorite books include:

Bunny Cakes by Rosemary Wells.
    Favorite cartoon rabbits Max and Ruby become bunnies who bake! Puffin (2000).

Chicken Soup with Rice: A Book of Months by Maurice Sendak.
 This classic book rhymes its way through each month, featuring the signature dish. HarperCollins (1991).

D.W. the Picky Eater by Marc Brown.
 Arthur's little sister doesn't like spinach but goes on an adventure that leads her to try more food choices! Little, Brown Books for Young Readers (1997).

Eating the Alphabet: Fruits & Vegetables from A to Z by Lois Ehlert.
 Wonderful pictures of fruits and vegetables for each letter of the alphabet. Sandpiper (1994).

Eating the Rainbow by Rena D. Grossman.
 Colorful pictures of babies and food. Star Bright Books (2009).

Gregory the Terrible Eater by Mitchell Sharmat.
 The tale of a goat who won't eat the stuff that's good for him! Scholastic Paperbacks (2009).

Growing Vegetable Soup by Lois Ehlert.
 This book details the raising of a vegetable garden and includes a great soup recipe. Sandpiper (1991).

Pie in the Sky by Lois Ehlert.
 The tale of a family who waits all year for their tree to produce bud, then flower, then fruit so they can make a delicious cherry pie to share with the birds. Harcourt Children's Books (2004).

Index

4/13 '5

About the Author

Gabrielle Kaplan-Mayer is a freelance writer, educator, and cooking instructor based in Philadelphia. The author of several nonfiction books for adults, including **Insulin Pump Therapy Demystified** and **The Creative Jewish Wedding Book,** she currently teaches a cooking class at Gratz College for teenagers who prepare meals for home-bound senior citizens. As a cooking instructor, she integrates students with special needs, including autism, Down syndrome, ADHD, and intellectual disabilities. The mother of two young children, including a son with autism, she enjoys cooking with them in her own kitchen classroom. Visit her at www.kitchenclassroom4kids.com!